Language Teaching:
A Scheme for Teacher Education

Editors: C N Candlin and H G Widdowson

Grammar

Rob Batstone

Oxford University Press

Oxford University Press
Walton Street, Oxford OX2 6DP

Oxford New York
Athens Auckland Bangkok Bombay
Calcutta Cape Town Dar es Salaam Delhi
Florence Hong Kong Istanbul Karachi
Kuala Lumpur Madras Madrid Melbourne
Mexico City Nairobi Paris Singapore
Taipei Tokyo Toronto

and associated companies in
Berlin Ibadan

OXFORD and OXFORD ENGLISH
are trade marks of Oxford University Press

ISBN 0 19 437132 8

© Oxford University Press 1994

First published 1994
Second impression 1995

No unauthorized photocopying

Typeset by Wyvern Typesetting Ltd, Bristol

Printed in Hong Kong

To my father

Contents

The author and series editors

Rob Batstone is a lecturer in Education at the University of London Institute of Education. He has worked as a teacher and teacher-trainer in the UK and abroad. In addition to grammar, he is interested in psycholinguistics and in aspects of discourse analysis. His Ph.D. research concerned relationships between grammar, lexis, and context.

Christopher N. Candlin is Professor and Chair of Linguistics in the School of English and Linguistics at Macquarie University, Sydney, and Executive Director of the National Centre for English Language Teaching and Research, having previously been Professor of Applied Linguistics and Director of the Centre for Language in Social Life at the University of Lancaster. He also co-founded and directed the Institute for English Language Education at Lancaster.

Henry Widdowson is Professor of English for Speakers of Other Languages at the University of London Institute of Education, and Professor of Applied Linguistics at the University of Essex. He was previously Lecturer in Applied Linguistics at the University of Edinburgh, and has also worked as an English Language Officer for the British Council in Sri Lanka and Bangladesh.

Through work with The British Council, The Council of Europe, and other agencies, both Editors have had extensive and varied experience of language teaching, teacher education, and curriculum development overseas, and both contribute to seminars, conferences, and professional journals.

Introduction

Grammar

Not long ago I was involved in a discussion amongst a group of language teachers. The talk centred on different kinds of teaching, and on the aspects of language which we were most concerned with as teachers. As you might expect, a fair number of topics were mentioned: 'discourse', 'vocabulary', 'reading', 'speaking', 'communication', and (last but not least) 'grammar'. When we talk in these very general terms about the practice of language teaching, it is hard to avoid carving things up into separate segments, each with its own label. But this kind of labelling can go too far, leading to a point where we misrepresent the nature of language and—in particular—the nature of grammar. In fact, grammar is part of discourse, an essential feature of reading and speaking, and is difficult to separate in any clear-cut way from vocabulary. Crucially, effective communication in a language would be seriously impaired without an ability to put grammar to use in a variety of situations.

When I began teaching, I remember leaving the classroom at the end of a lesson with the thought 'Well, today we did the first conditional' or 'That's the passive taken care of'. These days I am more cautious, and in this book I have tried to show that far from being a self-contained entity, grammar is an immensely pervasive phenomenon. It is an integral part of language, so that the more we can find out about how grammar is learned and used, the better placed we will be to teach it effectively.

I have been lucky in the support I have received during the writing of this book. Henry Widdowson has been a stimulating editor, and his confidence in me has always been a great encouragement. I am also grateful to Chris Candlin for his critical and helpful reading of the various manuscripts. Thanks also to Peter Skehan for his useful comments on a section of the book. Finally, I am grateful to many friends for their support. Thank you to Sybil, Steve, Robyn, Geoff, Janet, Anne, and Currie for your patience and fellowship, and for knowing when (and when not) to ask the question 'How's the book going?'

Rob Batstone

Language Teaching:
A Scheme for Teacher Education

The purpose of this scheme of books is to engage language teachers in a process of continual professional development. We have designed it so as to guide teachers towards the critical appraisal of ideas and the informed application of these ideas in their own classrooms. The scheme provides the means for teachers to take the initiative themselves in pedagogic planning. The emphasis is on critical enquiry as a basis for effective action.

We believe that advances in language teaching stem from the independent efforts of teachers in their own classrooms. This independence is not brought about by imposing fixed ideas and promoting fashionable formulas. It can only occur where teachers, individually or collectively, explore principles and experiment with techniques. Our purpose is to offer guidance on how this might be achieved.

The scheme consists of three sub-series of books covering areas of enquiry and practice of immediate relevance to language teaching and learning. Sub-series 1 (of which this present volume forms a part) focuses on areas of *language knowledge*, with books linked to the conventional levels of linguistic description: pronunciation, vocabulary, grammar, and discourse. Sub-series 2 focuses on different *modes of behaviour* which realize this knowledge. It is concerned with the pedagogic skills of speaking, listening, reading, and writing. Sub-series 3 focuses on a variety of *modes of action* which are needed if this knowledge and behaviour is to be acquired in the operation of language teaching. The books in this sub-series have to do with such topics as syllabus design, the content of language courses, and aspects of methodology and evaluation.

This sub-division of the field is not meant to suggest that different topics can be dealt with in isolation. On the contrary, the concept of a scheme implies making coherent links between all these different areas of enquiry and activity. We wish to emphasize how their integration formalizes the complex factors present in any teaching process. Each book, then, highlights a particular topic, but also deals contingently with other issues, themselves treated as focal in other books in the series. Clearly, an enquiry into a mode of behaviour like speaking, for example, must also refer to aspects of language knowledge which it realizes. It must also connect to modes of action which can be directed at developing this behaviour in learners. As elements of the whole scheme, therefore, books cross-refer both within and across the different sub-series.

This principle of cross-reference which links the elements of the scheme is also applied to the internal design of different inter-related books within it. Thus, each book contains three sections, which, by a combination of text and task, engage the reader in a principled enquiry into ideas and practices. The first section of each book makes explicit those theoretical ideas which bear on the topic in question. It provides a conceptual framework for those sections which follow. Here the text has a mainly *explanatory* function, and the tasks serve to clarify and consolidate the points raised. The second section shifts the focus of attention to how the ideas from Section One relate to activities in the classroom. Here the text is concerned with *demonstration*, and the tasks are designed to get readers to evaluate suggestions for teaching in reference both to the ideas from Section One and also to their own teaching experience. In the third section this experience is projected into future work. Here the set of tasks, modelled on those in Section Two, are designed to be carried out by the reader as a combination of teaching techniques and action research in the actual classroom. It is this section that renews the reader's contact with reality: the ideas expounded in Section One and linked to pedagogic practice in Section Two are now to be systematically *tested out* in the process of classroom teaching.

If language teaching is to be a genuinely professional enterprise, it requires continual experimentation and evaluation on the part of practitioners whereby in seeking to be more effective in their pedagogy they provide at the same time—and as a corollary—for their own continuing education. It is our aim in this scheme to promote this dual purpose.

Christopher N. Candlin
Henry Widdowson

Explanation
The nature of grammar

1 What is grammar?

1.1 Why grammar?

There is something distinctly familiar about grammar. Linguists have been studying it for centuries, and it remains an object of learning for countless schoolchildren the world over; it is an integral part of the language we use in everyday communication. Although we are probably not conscious of grammar in our own language use, as language teachers we can hardly fail to be aware of its influence. Grammar is a major influence in syllabus design, the focal point of many classroom exercises, and the key behind that familiar student query: 'Please, what is the rule here?'

But although grammar is familiar to us, precisely because of its familiarity it is sometimes difficult to stand back and take a clear look at it. To start at the beginning, then, what is grammar, and why should we concern ourselves with it? Language *without* grammar would certainly leave us seriously handicapped:

up and he that the in Bill Jane stand announce spring marry

As a piece of coherent English this awkward clutter of words is sadly lacking. And yet it is hard to resist the urge to reassemble these words so that, as with pieces of a jigsaw, plausible combinations begin to emerge out of the apparent chaos. One such combination could be:

Bill stand up announce that he and Jane marry in the spring

The question of how words can (or cannot) be combined in sentences is an important part of grammar, where it is the concern of *syntax*. By putting words together in this way, we have followed certain syntactic conventions for word order. We are also bringing meaning into a degree of focus; now we have some idea of what is going on here. But our understanding would be sharper if, for instance, this event was contextualized in time:

Bill *stood* up and announced that he and Jane *would* be marrying in the spring

Now our perception of things is clearer. Bill's significant announcement, it seems, occurred in the past, though his marriage to Jane is, as far as we know, an intention, not a matter of fact: he did not, for example, announce that he 'had married' Jane. To achieve this greater clarity, modifications have been made to the verbs—'stand' has become 'stood', 'marry' has been expanded into 'would be marrying'. Of course, these are not the only modifications which could be made: the verb 'stand' can be changed into 'stands' or 'standing'; and if we add in the auxiliary verbs, then we have 'might be standing', 'has stood', and a number of other options. Through grammar we can specify the ways in which words can be systematically modified through such alterations and additions. These modifications are part of *morphology*, and they help us to convey fundamental concepts like time, number, and gender. At its heart, then, grammar consists of two fundamental ingredients—syntax and morphology—and together they help us to identify grammatical forms which serve to enhance and sharpen the expression of meaning.

Language without grammar would be chaotic: countless words without the indispensable guidelines for how they can be ordered and modified. A study of grammar (syntax and morphology) reveals a structure and regularity which lies at the basis of language and enables us to talk of the 'language system'.

Just as it would be impossible to describe language without seeking out this underlying framework, so it would be impossible to learn a language effectively without drawing on grammar in some way. Indeed, many language learners enter classrooms with an acute awareness of the importance of grammar as a kind of framework through which they can structure their work, or measure their progress.

▶ TASK 1

A group of classroom learners were asked how an understanding of grammar might help them to learn English. What views of grammar emerge from these responses?

1 'Without learning grammar I wouldn't ever be able to speak English in a correct and accurate way.' (Sabine Gionini, Sweden)

2 'Out of school some time I feel shy to talk with people because I am afraid to do mistakes in grammar, so I rather not talk.' (Yamin Aglan, Qatar)

3 'When I write an essay I can use the right word in the proper place and I can use right tenses.' (Achara Boonruang, Thailand)

4 'I think that at first, when you know only how to say your name, your nationality, and that you're hungry, you don't need to know a lot of grammar. But going on learning English, you need to know the grammar to express yourself better.' (Giorgio Grillenoni, Italy)

1.2 Which grammar? product and process

The notion that language is not random but orderly is fundamental to any view of grammar. But beyond this, there is much more that we can say. Grammar is not a single, homogeneous 'object' but an immensely broad and diverse phenomenon. So before we move on, we will consider some further perspectives on grammar which are important for language teaching, and which will form the basis for much that follows.

Firstly, there is a distinction to be made between grammar as product and grammar as process. A *product* perspective on grammar is probably the most familiar to the majority of teachers. When we consult a grammar book we are likely to do so with certain expectations about how the material inside will be organized. The grammarian will have divided the language up in some way, with one chapter dealing with prepositional phrases and another with the verb phrase. Of course, grammarians will structure their material differently depending on their particular way of seeing things, some stressing the forms of the language system, others making meaning more prominent. Yet they have in common a perspective on grammar which is static. The emphasis is on the component parts of the language system, divided up into separate forms. Each form is the product of the grammarian's analysis, and this product perspective on grammar can be of great value to teachers and learners. By focusing on particular grammatical forms and their associated meanings, we can help learners to develop their knowledge of the grammatical system, and the meanings which it helps to signal.

But this process is only one side of the coin, because grammar is also a key element in the *process* of language use. When we talk of grammar as process, we are thinking of the myriad ways in which it is deployed from moment to moment in communication. Some understanding of grammar as process will be invaluable if we are to help learners to employ grammar effectively in their own language use. We cannot simply assume that because a learner has studied and practised the English first conditional, she will automatically be able to use it when she is busy navigating her way through the intricacies of real-time communication.

▶ TASK 2

Look at the following statements about grammar from teachers. Can you say whether a product or a process perspective is being taken in each case?

1 'In my classes students spend a lot of time solving problems in groups through discussion. I only step in when they call on me.'

2 'Well, today I did the past progressive. On Wednesday it's back to the passive.'

3 'Manuel's very keen. But when we have debates he gets really carried away and his language just goes to pieces.'

4 'Nadia is very slow to catch on in lessons. But after she's gone home and studied the summaries at the back of the book, she comes back to class and the difference is amazing.'

In this book we consider these perspectives on grammar, and assess their value for language teaching. We start (in 2 and 3) with grammar as product: we look at how grammar is divided up into separate forms, and at relationships between form and meaning. Then (in 4) we examine grammar as process, considering how language users call on grammar, why they do so, and, indeed, why they sometimes use very little grammar at all. Afterwards (in 5) we move on to consider the role of grammar in the processes of language learning, investigating how grammar emerges in learner language.

In Section Two we will look critically at how product and process perspectives can influence and facilitate the effective teaching of grammar.

2 Issues in grammatical description

2.1 Formal grammar and idealization

Our concern in **2** is with grammar as product, and with the many different ways in which grammatical forms and meanings can be represented. In **2.2** and **2.3** the focus is on meaning. Here, though, we are interested in the forms themselves—with what is called 'formal grammar'. Formal grammar deals with the mechanics of the language system. For instance, we can take a familiar item of grammatical description, such as 'subject', and strip away its connections with meaning (the 'doer' of action, etc.). This leaves us with a more abstract idea of what a subject is: it typically comes first in a statement, it is usually a noun, and so on.

In so saying, we have already hinted at a major issue in formal grammar; in using expressions such as 'typically' and 'usually' we are acknowledging that grammar is not a precise systematic framework. Unlike mathematics, where percentages and numbers have a fixed and utterly predictable role, grammar is something of a 'more or less' phenomenon, with some rules applying more consistently than others.

▶ TASK 3

Here are some well-known formal grammatical rules for English, though some apply more consistently than others. Which do you think is the most consistent, and which the least?

1 To form a third person singular in the present tense, add *-s* to the verb.

2 The subject precedes the verb.

3 To signal past tense with verbs, *-ed* is added after the verb stem. For example, *climb* becomes *climbed*.

4 The object comes after the verb.

Sometimes grammarians make very general statements about grammatical form—they will specify a finite list of possible formulations for the simple sentence (there are seven, and no others), they will tell us that verb phrases take either active or passive voice (and no other voices are possible), and so on. Such broad classifications bring a sense of security; this is how it is, the picture is clear. Yet when we turn to scrutinize actual sentences things are not so clear. We may even come across patterns

which are so particular that they appear immune to any kind of generalization or explanation. Why is it, for instance, that we can demonstrate
the passive with 'He was admired by Jane' but not 'He was fonded of by
Jane' (Newmeyer 1983:9)? Once we exemplify grammar through actual
instances we discover that grammar does not exist on its own. It is inter-
dependent with lexis, and in many cases grammatical regularity and
acceptability are constrained and conditioned by words. Thus, in morphology, the past morpheme *-ed* applies only where the verb in question
happens to be 'regular'.

When we make very general statements about grammar we are *idealizing*
about the language system, identifying broad patterns which effectively
conceal some of the less orderly grammatical facts of specific examples.
Nor is there anything very aberrant or unusual about this. It is similar
to the experience of air travel when, prior to landing, you glance out
of the plane's window to see an immaculate panorama of order: neat
demarcations between rural and urban areas bisected by vast and orderly
highways. This is the earth from 30 000 feet. Grammar at 30 000 feet
with its broad patterns—active, passive, and so on—looks similarly
ordered. But dip down to 10 000 feet and things begin to look quite
different: all that previous clarity and neatness is giving way to something
much denser and more complex—minor roads and sprawling conurba-
tions emerge revealing a clutter of detail. Grammar at 10 000 feet is
similarly cluttered, and marked by a lack of regularity.

We can think of this distinction—between broad idealizations and the
finer detail of actual instances—as a kind of scale or continuum.

More general level (30 000 feet)	Broad grammatical forms and categories e.g. subject–verb–object, active voice, passive voice
More specific level (10 000 feet)	Particular examples of grammatical forms, including lexis e.g. 'He was hit by a stone' (passive voice)

Figure 1

So, at a more detailed level we can discover how the particular choice of
words will limit the applicability of idealized grammatical rules. Typically, pedagogic grammars have used words as a means of illustrating
broad and idealized patterns, so that lexis is effectively subservient to
grammar. To some extent this is inevitable: grammarians aim to provide
a clear and economical account of language structure, and this means
that a fair degree of idealization is necessary. But we should not be
misled into thinking that 'grammar' is in any way an independent or
self-contained entity.

'The lexical system is not something that is fitted in afterwards to a set of slots defined by the grammar. The lexicon ... is simply the most delicate grammar ... as things become more and more specific, they tend more and more to be realized by the choice of a lexical item rather than the choice of a grammatical structure.'
(*Halliday 1978:43*)

The more sensitive our model of grammar, the more difficult it becomes to ignore this dependent relationship between grammar and lexis. Generative grammarians, for example, found it useful to take increasing account of lexis, and of the interactions between lexis and grammar, as they modified and elaborated their framework for grammatical description; see the discussion in Brown (1984).

▶ # TASK 4

How does the following extract help learners to consider grammar at 10 000 feet?

In four of the following sentences the Present Continuous is used incorrectly. Mark the four incorrect sentences with a cross.

a) Can you answer the phone? I'm having a bath.
b) I'm not understanding this exercise.
c) He's thinking about Helen. That's why he's sad.
d) She is liking the film.
e) They are watching television.
f) I am thinking English is a difficult language.
g) The seasons are changing four times a year.

(*Bell and Gower 1991:14*)

Of course, there *are* forms which behave in a completely rule-governed way. For example, the sequence of modal auxiliaries in the English verb phrase follows a strict and invariable rule. We can say, for instance, 'He would have been playing tennis' but not 'He have would been playing tennis'. Yet it would be a mistake to equate 'grammar' with 'absolute rule'. Regularity in language is a matter of degree; it would be more precise to talk of rules hedged about by conditions—conditions which in many cases depend on lexis as much as on grammar.

Learners who persist in expecting the target language to be strictly rule-governed will get 'derailed' on encountering exceptions. Certainly many learners do begin by making their own very broad idealizations about language, over-applying 'rules' and operating, in effect, with a simplified system which is pitched very much at 30 000 feet if not higher. They may, for instance, convert all verbs into the past by the simple addition of the *-ed* suffix, riding roughshod over distinctions between regular and irregular verbs.

▶ TASK 5

To what extent could you refer to a clear 'rule' in explaining the following learner errors?

1 she has three childs
2 came that man to my shop
3 I enjoy to play with my daughter
4 she was photograph by her uncle

Formulating such idealizations is a necessary first step in language learning: the reality of the target language is immensely complex and it will take time before learners can come to grips with many of its inconsistencies. The process of learning grammar will involve a progressive shift from more to less idealized notions of how grammar works: in other words, a gradual 'descent' from more to less idealization, as we shall see in greater detail in 5.3.

2.2 Grammar for meaning

▶ TASK 6

Below are three possible ways of dividing up a sentence into constituent parts. Which of the three options makes most sense, and how might you classify each sentence part using grammatical terminology?

1 [that] [man standing over] [there hates my] [dog]
2 [that man standing over there] [hates] [my dog]
3 [that man] [standing over] [there hates] [my dog]

The process whereby the grammarian analyses a sentence into its constituents may seem far removed from the 'real world': formulae and tree diagrams proliferate and at first sight we appear to be closer to mathematics than to meaningful language. Yet in Task 6 there is only one sensible option we could choose: the one which somehow feels right. In fact we could never hope to determine what goes together with what in syntax without drawing, at least in part, on our intuitions about meaning— about events, objects, participants, and relationships between them. The word *syntax* comes from the Greek and means 'a setting out together', and 'togetherness', putting together what we perceive to belong together, is a principle which lies at the heart of syntax (Bolinger 1975:136–7).

A study of grammar can also reveal how language itself has evolved over time, and how the needs of language users have shaped the language system into a communicative device which serves their purposes remarkably well. In order to survive, human beings have always had to meet certain fundamental needs, including the need to get things done, and to exchange basic information about the world around them. Grammar has evolved so that these needs can be expressed efficiently: interrogatives and affirmatives facilitate the exchange of information through question and statement, while the imperative mood provides a convenient means for the issuing of instructions and commands. Grammar is not simply a formal network, but a communicative device which is 'functionally motivated' (see the discussion in Halliday 1985: XIII–XXXV).

Many formal grammatical patterns can be reformulated, and expressed as generalizations about meaning. For example, the pattern 'subject–verb–indirect object–direct object' reflects a typical way of observing the world, loosely paraphrased as 'a relationship between a sender (or source) and a receiver where something is conveyed from the one to the other' as with 'Pass me the salt' and 'Felicity shot me a ferocious look'. Quite logically, grammar has evolved to facilitate the expression of basic meanings which are intrinsic to human life; meanings which are so indispensable and so commonly occurring that we require an economical means of expressing them. It would be patently absurd if we had to elaborate entirely new strings of words whenever we wanted to formulate a question, or observe events around us.

2.3 Grammar, meaning, and idealization

Just as with formal grammar, there is a scale here which takes us from the dizzy heights of vast generalization through to very particular examples. We can take the passive as an example. At a more general level, all we can say is something like: 'The passive allows us to omit the agent, making the receiver or "undergoer" into the subject' as in 'The wall was demolished', 'Cedric is overwhelmed by your kindness', and so on. Like all good idealizations, this serves us pretty well as a broad overview. But then we can shift down a few thousand feet, until we are close enough to ground level to observe this form in use in actual situations. We might chance to hear the passive used, say, in a domestic scene: two people survey the state of the flat they share; from time to time one or the other can be heard saying things like 'That electricity bill's not been paid yet' and 'The windows haven't been cleaned for months!' Now we have a real context in sight with actual individuals, their attitudes, and their relationships in focus, so that we can say more about how the passive can be used in context. By not referring directly to the agent of the action, the speaker can try to avoid claiming responsibility, or try to shift responsibility onto another person. 'The bill's not been paid' might mean something like 'It needs paying, but I'm not going to pay it!'. This scale of idealization is represented in Figure 2.

More general level (30 000 feet)	Broad meanings underlying very general patterns e.g. subject–verb–object, etc.

Generalizations about the meaning of particular forms e.g. passive, past tense, progressive |
| Less general level (10 000 feet) | Meanings signalled across a limited range of examples in contexts of use e.g. 'The passive *may* be used to disclaim responsibility in certain circumstances' |
| Actual instances (ground level) | Very specific and context-particular meanings signalled from moment to moment in language use |

Figure 2

▶ TASK 7

Here are some extracts from a pedagogic grammar. Each extract is a different kind of statement about the progressive form. How idealized is each one?

Normally, if something continues for a long time, it is no longer temporary: it is a state or a habit, and we use the Present Simple [see PRESENT SIMPLE 2a, 2b].

Compare: *We're living* in a small $\left\{ \begin{array}{l} \textit{apartment} <\text{U.S.}> \\ \textit{flat} <\text{mainly G.B.}> \end{array} \right\}$ *(at present).*
We (normally) live in a village near Rome.

However, we can use the Progressive for a habit if it is temporary.

E.g.   *She's **travelling** to work by bicycle while the bus strike is on.*
   *Margot **was working** in a night club when she was noticed by the manager of a West End theatre. Soon after that, she **was appearing** regularly on the West End stage.*

We can also use the Progressive for annoying habits [see PRESENT TIME 5a] with **always**.

E.g.   *You're **always interrupting** when I talk.*
   *She **was always running** away from home and **being brought** home by the police.*

Here the habit is not temporary: it goes on and on!

> The **Progressive** form of the verb phrase contains a form of the verb
> BE + the -ING FORM:
>
> BE a Verb-**ing** E.g. $\left\{\begin{array}{l} \textbf{\textit{is}} \\ \textbf{\textit{was}} \end{array}\right\} \left\{\begin{array}{l} \textbf{\textit{coming}} \\ \textbf{\textit{looking}} \end{array}\right.$

> The **Progressive** form usually describes a temporary happening, i.e.
> something which happens during a limited period.

(*Leech 1989:390–4*)

Sometimes learners are given idealizations which are simply wrong. This happens most often with prescriptive statements about grammar, statements which tell us under which conditions a form may or may not be used. There was a time, for example, when almost all pedagogic grammars provided rules for the use of *some* and *any* along the following lines:

'*Some* is for affirmative sentences. *Any* is used with interrogatives and negatives. The exception is when we use an interrogative in making offers or requests, where we can use *some*, e.g. *Would you like some more coffee?*'

With the help of computers, we are now able to undertake large-scale surveys of language as it is actually used, and to reformulate some (or any) ill-conceived idealizations. One such program has revealed beyond all doubt that the above regulation for *some* and *any* is incorrect, and that 'the use of *any* in an affirmative sentence is in fact much commoner than its use in interrogatives' (Willis 1990:49) as with 'Anything you can do I can do better' or 'Any fool knows that!'

Prescriptive statements about grammar are relatively easy to evaluate and to reformulate; they deal with verifiable facts about grammar, and very often they turn out to be either right or wrong. Things are somewhat less straightforward when we turn to look more directly at meaning. If we were to say 'the present tense is used for talking about present time', we would, of course, be making a vast idealization which would be of little practical value. The present tense can signal future time, as with 'When he *arrives* I'll speak to him', and even past time, as with 'At the bus-stop, this man *comes* up to me and he *says*...'. So there are good grounds for giving our idealizations a sharper focus. But how sharply focused should they be? Take, for instance, the progressive form. It is commonly said that the progressive describes 'something which happens during a limited period' (Leech 1989:390). This formulation appears to be considerably sharper than the aforementioned equation between present tense and present time. Yet we can still find counter-examples. What about 'We're all getting older'? Sadly, this is a process which continues unabated: it is not (except in the bleakest sense) a 'limited period'. And

how about 'She's always buying me presents'? Here, again, the idealization is inadequate: we are talking about a repeated event which, particularly with the word 'always' attached, is seen to be ongoing beyond a
limited period.

But we can go too far in a quest for accuracy, engaging in an ongoing
process of formulation and reformulation, as counter-examples and more
finely tuned accounts follow each other in an endless pursuit for the
perfect idealization. But there is no such thing. All that can happen is
that we get so close to 'ground level' that we end up observing details of
language as they emerge utterance by utterance. In the domestic scene
we visited earlier, it may be that 'The windows haven't been cleaned for
months!' was uttered with a genuine intention to cause embarrassment
or hurt. Yet it would appear odd to assert that 'the passive can be used
to cause embarrassment or hurt in domestic conflicts concerning the
cleaning of windows'! Once we reach ground level, the grammarian
ceases to exist, because grammar is of its nature a way of identifying
what is typical or recurring across instances, both of form and of meaning. Human language is not artificial; it has evolved gradually, so that it
is full of categories with fuzzy boundaries, with no clear dividing line
between grammar and lexis. When we give clear-cut idealizations to our
learners, we are (of necessity) being economical with the truth.

▶ TASK 8

According to one much-used source, the past simple and past continuous tenses 'convey the idea that the action in the past continuous started before the action in the simple past and probably continued after it' (Thomson and Martinet 1986:163–4). They
provide the following illustration:

When I arrived

Tom was talking on the phone

(*Thomson and Martinet 1986:163*)

How well does this idealization cope with the following examples?
Do you think that Thomson and Martinet's formulation is
adequate to cover the majority of instances?

1 When I shot him, Tom was talking on the phone.
2 When I arrived, my husband was standing on the table dancing
   the tango. He stopped at once and gave me a sheepish look.
3 Sheila was watching TV when the power-cut came.

4 I was thinking of going out for a walk when I suddenly remembered the fish in the oven...

Would you want to reformulate Thomson and Martinet's statement to account for these examples?

There is no absolute litmus test for deciding whether or not Thomson and Martinet's formulation is right or wrong. But it is important to remain alert to the issues involved in idealization, and—in language teaching—to be sensitive to the learner's perspective. On the one hand, we will want to avoid proliferating such subtle distinctions of meaning that learners cannot see the wood for the trees. On the other hand, we should avoid providing idealizations which are so insensitively formulated that learners just cannot relate them to actual examples which they encounter.

3 Distance and attitude: grammar in context

3.1 Grammar, choice, and point of view

The foregoing discussion has been concerned largely with grammar and meaning at a high level of generalization: with heavy-duty idealizations and with the factors involved in their formulation. Such idealizations abound in language teaching materials. Yet while there are, as we have seen, arguments in favour of broad idealizations, we should also consider diversifying. In **2.3** it was noted that the passive may be used to avoid and to shift responsibility as with 'These windows haven't been cleaned for ages'. This function of the passive does not emerge from broader idealizations. Azar, for instance, notes only that it is 'most frequently used when it is not known or not important to know *exactly* who performs an action' (1985:125). Of course, shifting responsibility is not something which the passive always signals; it is a function which we will encounter only in *some* contexts of use. It is grammar at 10 000 feet, occupying a middle ground between large-scale idealizations and the very finely tuned meanings which we will always encounter on specific occasions (see Figure 2).

This middle ground is worth investigating further. When we communicate through language we do not simply pick grammatical items off the shelf, packaged with ready-made meanings. We fashion and *choose* language to express ourselves, conveying a particular point of view. It is not only grammar which enables us to do this. But grammar is, none the less, important in helping speakers to situate themselves in relation to the world around them. This more context-sensitive account of grammar is the subject of **3.2**, and we will investigate it by focusing in particular on two of the best-known idealizations: the present tense and the past tense. Can we identify ways in which these forms are used which reveals something not visible at 30 000 feet?

3.2 Social distance

Grammar has evolved to help us to function effectively in social life. In fact, it is hard to disentangle grammar from the very processes of socialization which we take for granted. To co-operate effectively in groups, we need both to get things done in our own interests, and also to attend to the needs and wishes of others. In making a request, for example, there is always a potential conflict between these two needs: we want something for ourselves, but how can we meet our own needs without appearing to threaten the needs, or the 'face' of the other person? Every request is potentially face-threatening. Language has evolved to give us conventional ways of handling this potential conflict. We routinely say things like 'Could I . . . ?' or 'Would you mind . . . ?', suggesting (at least in theory) that what we want will depend on the other's willingness to cooperate (Brown and Levinson 1983); in short, language used for politeness. When we use language to signal this kind of attention to face, we convey a sense of respectful distance between ourselves and our interlocutor. In signalling different degrees of directness or intimacy we are giving expression to what is known as 'social distance'.

▶ **TASK 9**

Can you sequence the following ways of making a request so that they are in order of increasing politeness?

1 £20!

2 I was wondering if it might be possible for you to lend me £20.

3 Can you lend me £20?

4 Could you lend me £20?

5 Lend me £20.

Notice how past and present forms get used here. When we signal a degree of social distance, we may do so by using present forms, as with 'Can you . . . ?' When we step up the social distance and signal greater politeness, we switch to past forms, as with 'I was wondering . . .', 'Could you . . . ?'. The more polite and socially distant, the more likely it is that we will shift from present to past forms.

And yet 'present' and 'past' are not the right terms. These are words we use to talk about time, not politeness. But there *is* a connection which has to do with distance. The past is distant from us, the present is close, just as great politeness is seen as being distant and directness as being close. There is, so to speak, *temporal* distance between present and past, as there is *social* distance between being polite and being direct. What happens, it seems, is that we use these present and past forms in a number of different yet related ways.

As teachers we can consider the language of politeness in one of two ways. On the one hand, we might say these are essentially familiar expressions for doing useful things with language, and so we should teach them as such: as independent chunks, each of which can be separately taught. This is a common approach in language teaching, where functional expressions are presented as fixed phrases, with little or no highlighting of their grammatical constituents. This is a kind of lexical approach, in which language is revealed as an inventory of expressions, as if they were extended lexical items. In contrast, we could encourage learners to make generalizations across these expressions, generalizations which have to do with past and present forms and with the various connections between form and meaning which we have been examining. This would be a more grammatical approach. There is no reason why both approaches should not be pursued, at different times.

▶ TASK 10

Which of these two approaches—lexical or grammatical—seems to be taken in the following extract from a pedagogic grammar?

ASKING FOR PERMISSION: *MAY I, COULD I, CAN I*

POLITE QUESTION	POSSIBLE ANSWERS	
(a) **May I** please borrow your pen? (b) **Could I** please borrow your pen? (c) **Can I** please borrow your pen?	Yes. Yes. Of course. Yes. Certainly. Of course. Certainly. Sure. (*informal*) Okay. (*informal*) Uh-huh. (*meaning* yes)	People use **may I, could I,*** and **can I** to ask polite questions. The questions ask for someone's permission. (a), (b), and (c) have basically the same meaning. Note: **can I** is less formal than **may I** and **could I**.
		Please can come at the end of the question: *May I borrow your pen, please?* **Please** can be omitted from the question: *May I borrow your pen?*

* In a polite question, **could** is not the past form of **can**.

(*Azar 1985:59*)

Another way of 'keeping our distance' when we want something done is to avoid naming the person we want to do it. We have already encountered an example of this (2.3) with the passive. When someone says 'The windows haven't been cleaned for months', it is likely to be clear what they mean—'I'm not cleaning them! How about you?'—and yet they cannot strictly be held accountable: 'What? No, I'm not saying that you should do it. I'm just making an observation'. The passive, that is, enables us to refer to events without acknowledging the agent responsible for them, thereby creating a sense of distance between events and their sources.

▶ TASK 11

Which forms are being used to signal distance in the following examples?

1 I suppose you couldn't stay on a bit longer?

2 By the way, the fridge needs cleaning.

3 You couldn't lend me your tape-recorder, could you?

3.3 Psychological distance

Consider the following exchange between two friends:

Bill: Hey, have you been watching the re-run of that comedy series on TV—*Fresno*, I think it's called?

Tom: Ah, *Fresno*, yes! Annabelle really loves that programme.

Bill: Look, Tom. I'm sorry but you really must let go of Annabelle. She left you over two years ago, for goodness sake!

When Tom says 'Annabelle really loves that programme' he is using the present tense because his memory of Annabelle is still very much a reality. She is still a part of Tom's subjective 'here and now'—out of sight, perhaps, but not out of mind. If Tom had been able to come to terms with the loss of Annabelle, then he might have said (much more dispassionately) 'She loved that programme', using the past tense to signal that both objectively and subjectively the relationship was truly in the past.

So the choice of past or present forms can be influenced by subjective perspectives on events. We might use present forms when we feel psychologically that they are still close to us, still relevant to us, and part of our current mental world. Conversely, we can use past forms when the experiences we refer to are perceived as complete, as no longer relevant, and therefore at some distance from the point to which we have now moved on. We can refer to this as 'psychological distance'.

The grammatical signalling of psychological distance may be used for a variety of purposes. Sometimes, as in the case of Tom and Annabelle, it serves to reveal something of the speaker's state of mind, and something of how he positions himself in relation to others. On other occasions it will be used rather less introspectively, in order to impress a certain viewpoint on the reader or listener. In the following passage, for example, the writer uses past and present tenses to convey a very particular way of regarding two contrasting schools of thought:

'Skinner (1957) <u>argued</u> that language <u>was</u> learned through a process of *stimulus–response*, with large amounts of controlled repetition. Chomsky (1959) <u>argues</u> that language could never be learned in this way, and that we <u>are</u> all endowed at birth with a *language acquisition device* which <u>provides</u> essential assistance in the learning process.'
(*Adapted from Riddle 1986:269*)

▶ **TASK 12**

1 How exactly is the writer in the passage above exploiting grammar to signal psychological distance? How common do you think this pattern of language use is, and would you consider introducing it to learners at any point?

2 It is not only through grammar that such meanings are expressed. Very often grammar and lexis function in alliance to reinforce a certain viewpoint. How is this achieved in the following examples?

– Skinner (1957) <u>claimed</u> that language was learned...
– Chomsky (1959) <u>demonstrates</u> that language could never...

The text in the examples in question 2 of Task 12 is the language of reported speech. For many years, grammarians have told us that there are clear rules for the formulation of reported speech, governing the choice of tense in the verbs used. For example:

When the 'reporting' verb is past (eg *she said*; *I thought*; *we wondered*; *Max wanted to know*), we do not normally use the same tenses as the original speaker.

The verbs are 'more past' (because we are not talking at the same time as the speaker was). Compare:

direct speech	**reported speech**
present simple 'I **like** peaches.'	past simple He said he **liked** peaches.
present progressive '**Is** it raining?'	past progressive He asked if it **was** raining.
past simple 'I **didn't** recognize you.'	past perfect She explained that she **hadn't** recognized me.
present perfect '**You've** annoyed the dog.'	past perfect I told her **she'd** annoyed the dog.
past progressive 'I **was** joking about the price.'	past perfect progressive He said he **was** joking (or: **had been** joking) about the price.

(Swan 1980:534/5)

An over-rigorous application of such accounts can create the impression that reported speech is a matter of acting on fixed syntactic principles and of providing an objective or faithful record of what was said. It is very much a '30 000 feet idealization', and it has been the subject of considerable criticism (see, for example, Harman 1990; Yule, Mathis, and Hopkins 1992). It contrasts sharply with the way forms are deployed in Task 12, which is much more specific to a particular context. But there are arguments on both sides. Swan's presentation has the great benefit of clarity, and surely there must be many occasions when it works well enough. The text in Task 12 reveals something quite different about reported speech, but it is grammar at 10 000 feet, so that inevitably its application is more limited. We are saying merely that there are conventions for the signalling of attitude which we can generalize about to some extent. We should, perhaps, give a more refined and contextualized account of such forms to more experienced learners, while keeping things relatively clear for lower-level learners. In effect, this would mean providing higher-level idealizations for lower-level learners, and lower-level idealizations for higher-level learners.

3.4 Hypothetical distance

It is a distinctive feature of human language that we can use it to create imaginary worlds. Thus we can invent fictional pasts, and talk about possible or impossible futures. Grammar gives us the forms to do this, including future forms and the various past tenses. But we create worlds not solely to describe past and future.

▶   TASK 13

1 What meanings are being signalled in the following by past and past perfect tenses?
   – If I *was* famous I'*d* feel very exposed. I *could* never escape.
   – Isn't it time you *were* in bed?
   – If only I *hadn't* said that!
   – If I *were* you, I'*d* think very carefully before making a decision.
   – *Hadn't* you better leave?   ˋ

2 The next two examples show how grammar and lexis function together in the creation of particular meanings. In terms of time reference, what effect does the change of lexical item have?
   – If I *earned* £50 000, I'd be completely happy.
   – If I *won* £50 000, I'd be completely happy.

Many of these functions are quite commonplace in existing teaching materials: 'expressing regret and wishes', 'giving advice', and so on. Underlying them, there is a common grammatical thread. Past forms are being used to signal 'hypothetical distance': the distance between the tangible, real world and the created world of our own imagination. We can express this distance in a variety of ways: we prefer a certain unreal world to circumstances as they are (regret), or we signal that the unreal world will soon become a reality unless certain conditions are met (warn, threaten), and so on. Typically, textbooks and pedagogic grammars present this kind of material in separate chapters or units, one dealing with 'wishes' and another with 'threats'. But as was argued with respect to social

distance, there is a case for making learners aware of this common grammatical thread, thereby enabling them to formulate useful generalizations
across a range of expressions.

3.5 Grammar and distance in review

By examining grammar as it is used in context, we can begin to identify
meanings which are not apparent at 30 000 feet.

	Distant	**Here-and-now**
Temporal distance (time)	past, future (*past tense, future forms*)	present (*present tense*)
Social distance	being polite, avoiding intrusion into listener's territory (*past tense*) avoiding 'naming' to control or to avoid responsibility (*passive voice*)	being direct (e.g. imperative forms) explicitly 'naming' the agent or doer of an action (*active voice*)
Psychological distance	considered outside current mental world (*past tense*)	considered relevant to current mental world (*present tense*)
Hypothetical distance	unlikely or unreal worlds (*past, past perfect tenses*)	real and actual worlds (*present tense*)

Figure 3

▶   TASK 14

How clearly does the following account of the past tense deal
with these issues, conveying a more context-sensitive impression
of grammar? It comes from a pedagogic grammar 'for advanced
students'. Do you feel that these are matters which should only be
revealed to more advanced learners? Would you want to modify
it in any way for a particular group of learners?

But just as the present simple refers to events other than present ones, so the past simple is used to refer to events other than past. Thus we use it to refer to the present and occasionally the future when a verb is back-shifted in indirect speech, in wishing and hypothetical clauses. We also use it referring to the present time for the purpose of distancing ourselves.

Past events, states and habits
The event or state may be short or long, and a number of happenings in the distant past may be thought of as a single event.

> I **was** scared stiff that night.
> I **knew** your mother well.
> The gate **led** into the lane.
> He never **let** himself become excited by ... danger.
> A plover **called** three or four times and was silent.

Back-shift

> It's time we **got** back.   [after *it's time ...*]
> I wish it **would** rain.   [after *wish*]
> Still, he thought, this **was** no time to pick and choose.
>   [indirect speech]
> I wouldn't care if my legs **weren't** so tired.   [in hypothetical clause]

We sometimes use a simple past form to refer to the present time as a marker of social distance or politeness:

> **Could** you just go and try the rope, Hazel?
> You **wanted** me, Hazel?

These are alternatives for the less polite/deferential *Can you just go ...?*
You want me?

(*Broughton 1990:211*)

3.6 Conclusions

'That's another thing we've learned from *your* Nation', said Mein Herr, 'map making. But we've carried it much further than *you*. What do you consider the *largest* map that would be really useful?'
'About six inches to the mile.'
'Only *six inches*!' exclaimed Mein Herr. 'We very soon got to six *yards* to the mile. Then we tried a *hundred* yards to the mile. And then came the grandest idea of all! We actually made a map of the country, on the scale of a *mile to a mile*!'
'Have you used it much?' I enquired.
'It has never been spread out, yet,' said Mein Herr: 'the farmers objected: they said it would cover the whole country, and shut out the sunlight! So we now use the country itself, as its own map, and I assure you it does nearly as well.'
(Lewis Carroll: *Sylvie and Bruno Concluded*)

Grammar is the great systematizing force of language, allowing us to be endlessly creative with a finite set of resources. But we can represent this system more or less broadly, using idealizations which are more or less finely tuned. For learners, idealizations provide a rough-and-ready map which sketches out some of the main routes through the tricky terrain of forms and their meanings. A map which is too detailed will confuse the learner and thus fail in its primary purpose: to be a guide. But a map which is too idealized will fare no better. Learners will become derailed on encountering landmarks which were not marked—discovering, that is, so many exceptions that the map becomes an obstacle to further learning. In teaching we need to ensure that learners are not seriously misled in either of these ways. Of course, we cannot be expected to provide learners with weekly maps which are perfectly judged to meet their precisely calculated needs. But we can ensure that learners are given a variety of indicators, and that we do not ignore a more representative perspective—grammar at 10 000 feet.

4   Language use: grammar as process

4.1 Introduction

Up to this point we have concentrated on a *product* view of grammar.
We have, in other words, been isolating particular forms, regarding them
first in terms of form and then in terms of meaning. The key word here,
though, is 'isolating', for in both cases we have sealed grammar off from
the cut and thrust of communication as an ongoing *process*. Of course,
there is much that we can learn about grammar as product by examining
its component parts. But then what happens when these parts are put
together moment-by-moment in language use? What does grammar
enable us to do with language as we build up stretches of dynamic discourse in speech and in writing? An understanding of these issues can
help us to guide learners sensitively to use grammar in ongoing
communication.

4.2 Grammar and knowledge of the world

An alien from a distant galaxy is planning a visit to Planet Earth. It
knows nothing of human cultures and it has never heard any human
language being spoken. So as light reading during its long voyage it
procures a book with the significant title *English Syntactic Structures*: a
comprehensive formal grammar. On finally landing (in Piccadilly Circus)
it is well versed in the formal regulations governing syntax and morphology, and feels ready for its first close encounter with human beings. It
is approached by a human clutching an empty bottle and an unlit cigarette, who addresses it with the words 'Got a light, mate?' The alien is
stunned into inevitable silence. It understands precisely nothing. What
on earth does this language mean?

This alien had a problem which reveals something crucial about language
in use. A thorough knowledge of the formal grammatical system is not
sufficient to enable us to communicate. We also need a knowledge of the
world so that we can make sense both *of* language and *with* language.
To understand 'Got a light?' we need to know roughly what a cigarette
is, that some people smoke them, that cigarettes need to be lit, and that
it is not unheard of for strangers to request a light in a public place. To
put language to use, then, we require two kinds of knowledge, known
respectively as *schematic knowledge* (knowledge of the world) and *systemic knowledge* (knowledge of the language system).

What counts, though, is the way in which systemic and schematic knowledge work together. Language does not simply make sense as a self-contained system; rather, we make sense of language by utilizing our world knowledge. Indeed, if we could not take a fair amount of schematic knowledge for granted, we would find ourselves in the cumbersome position of having to spell out a great deal which we conventionally take for granted, as in 'I had a bath this morning, by which I mean that I first turned on the tap, a tap being a metallic object...'. What happens, of course, is that we routinely assume a degree of shared schematic knowledge, and we adjust what we say accordingly (see pages 68–75 of Cook: *Discourse*, published in this Scheme). If we can safely assume that our listener has a fair amount of relevant schematic knowledge, then it would be pointless and perhaps confusing for us to spell things out in this clumsy way. There is a kind of trade-off struck between language and shared schematic knowledge; the more knowledge is shared, the less need to elaborate through language.

▶ TASK 15

How much schematic knowledge does the speaker assume is shared in the following examples?

1 The red one please, John. Thanks.

2 Sorry, but I wonder whether you could just go across the corridor into the main office opposite the lift. I need a large red file which has a big label on it saying 'Urgent'. It's in the corner of the room by the big plant, next to a blue file which says 'Students' on it. Is that clear?

3 Red file!

This book began with two questions about the nature of grammar: 'Why grammar?' (**1.1**) and 'Which grammar?' (**1.2**). Here a third question is considered: 'How much grammar?' How much grammar we use at any particular time will depend in large part on how much shared knowledge we can assume our interlocutor has, and the balance will shift from time to time. In **4.3** we look at cases where grammar is used minimally or not at all. In **4.4** we consider the other side of this coin, examining contexts where grammar is needed. These are important questions. The better we can understand the contexts in which grammar is deployed more or less extensively, the better placed we will be to construct classroom contexts and tasks to motivate an appropriate use of grammar by learners—as we shall see later, in **8**.

4.3 Grammar and shared knowledge: redundancy

The convention that we adjust what we say to take account of shared knowledge is such a powerful one that forms have evolved precisely for this purpose. Some of the so-called grammar words, including auxiliaries and determiners such as *this* and *that*, allow us to refer to something briefly, because (given what our interlocutor knows) it would be uneconomical to elaborate any further. Sometimes we will refer back to something already mentioned, as with 'I really enjoyed myself today.' 'Did you?', where the auxiliary 'did' clearly refers to 'enjoyed myself today'. On other occasions we may refer out of the text altogether, to something which we simply assume will be understood. We might say 'I went to the garage. They were really rude', where 'they' presumably refers to the garage staff. Using such forms appropriately, we can make our language hang together by signalling all kinds of references across sentence boundaries, giving language greater *cohesion* (see Cook: *Discourse*, pages 14–22).

Such language serves a communicative, economizing purpose, and it extends into other areas of the grammar. One form whose communicative potential is often overlooked is the negative. Take the following exchange:

Jane: Hi Harry. How's life?
Harry: Well, it's been better. I'm not going to Rio.

The negative in 'I'm not going to Rio' evokes considerable background knowledge which Harry assumes to be shared. He estimates, in other words, that Jane knows that he had been hoping to go to Rio. Yet none of this is said: the negative form is all that is needed to counter a prior expectation, and negative forms are so commonly used to do this that we almost need to think twice about it before we can see it at work (Givon 1979b:103).

▶   **TASK 16**

How are the italicized forms in the following examples being used to account for shared knowledge?

1 **A:** Did you see Geoff playing cricket when you were in Sydney last week?
   B: I *did*.

2 Tape-recording on a telephone answering machine:
   'I'm sorry but I'm *not* here to take your call right now...'

3 **A:** I really believe that the more we eat the better we feel.
   B: *That's* weird!

4 Young child standing on the edge of a diving board:
   'I *can't* do *it*!'

It is not just that we reduce our call on grammar in reference to shared knowledge. Sometimes we abandon grammar altogether. A friend recently attended a conference and found himself, one lunchtime, seated opposite two people who appeared to know each other well and who were engrossed in conversation. Having waited politely for a suitable pause in their discussion, he introduced himself and enquired their opinion of that morning's proceedings. Their responses (let us call them **A** and **B**) took him somewhat by surprise:

A: Well?
B: Hmmm. Yes. Interesting.

After this they continued with their previous discussion, as if the interruption had never occurred. **A** and **B** had evidently built up a degree of shared knowledge which enabled them to talk in this brief way. In fact, it is possible that they were exploiting their shared knowledge in order to deliberately exclude an outsider, effectively utilizing language (or the lack of it) in the exercise of power. This tells us something very significant about grammar as process: we don't always need it. Or to be more precise, there are occasions when language users will already share sufficient knowledge for grammatical elaboration to be redundant. Quite often, words will do adequately enough on their own as with 'Hmmm. Yes. Interesting'.

Sometimes shared knowledge will be so extensive that there is actually no need for language at all. When two mountaineers stand on the summit of Mount Everest and survey the panorama around them, it would sound trite to say 'Well, we've been through a lot, haven't we?', or 'Looks nice, doesn't it?'. The context speaks for itself, so that a shared smile or a handclasp might 'say it all'.

There are no rules here, but a pattern which helps us to understand grammar in use: the less we can account for shared knowledge, the more we need to call on grammar. The more shared knowledge we can assume, the more we can shift from grammar to lexis. Ultimately, we may move out of the language system altogether, communicating non-verbally through gesture and sign (as with the mountaineers). There is a scale in operation:

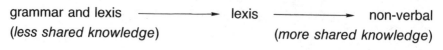

grammar and lexis ⟶ lexis ⟶ non-verbal
(less shared knowledge)   *(more shared knowledge)*

Figure 4

▶ TASK 17

In what kind of context do you imagine the following exchanges taking place? What degree of shared knowledge is being assumed in each case, and can you say where you would locate each exchange on the scale in Figure 4?

1 **A:** Coffee?
  B: Mmmmmm...

2 **A:** Dad, erm...?
  B: For the last time, no!

3 **A:** (Nods)
  B: £10 000 from the lady in the corner with the large hat.

This is grammar as an integral part of the process of language use, a resource which is activated more or less depending on context. But the word 'grammar' is itself a noun, and nouns, as the old idealization goes, refer to 'objects', a distinctly static concept. To better capture the dynamism of grammar as process, we will add in a verbal element and talk of the process of *grammaticization*. Language users choose how much to grammaticize according to the situation and their assumptions about how much their knowledge is shared (Rutherford 1987).

This 'more or less' quality to grammar as process applies not only to language producers, but also to listeners and readers. When we pick up a newspaper, we may begin by reading the headline and the first few lines in order to gather a general impression of what the text is about. Having done that, we may well find ourselves skipping through subsequent detail. We manage this because we have engaged our schematic knowledge, building up expectations about the article's content which will reduce our dependence on the details of the text itself. Just as in language production, readers and listeners will attend more or less extensively to grammar depending on how much shared knowledge there is. Again, there is a kind of scale here extending from grammar to lexis. Encountering an unfamiliar text may mean having to attend quite closely to its content, including its grammar. But given a sufficient degree of shared knowledge, we will shift our attention much more to lexis. Consider, for instance, the following text:

'Anne ambled through the garden. The flowers were stunning. Then she noticed that the roses were being watered by a small boy with long hair...'

Once it becomes apparent that this narrative is in the past, it becomes unnecessary to continue to attend to the past forms. The passive is similarly redundant. There is only one logical way in which 'flowers', 'water', and 'boy' are likely to link up: only in the most peculiar fantasy world would we find small boys being watered by flowers. So the reader might glide over much of the grammar here, attending instead to the key lexical

items. Reading in this way, and applying appropriate schematic knowledge, the text appears clear enough:

'Anne – amble – garden. Flowers – stunning. Notice – roses – water –
small boy – long hair . . .'

This tendency to pay less attention to the linguistic detail of texts (and
to grammar in particular) when context and relevant knowledge of the
world can be exploited is called *top-down processing*.

4.4 Needing grammar: unshared knowledge

But enough about the redundancy of grammar. Examples like the one
above need to be measured against the multitude of texts which require
considerable attention to grammar:

'Anne *had ambled* through the garden. The flowers *weren't* stunning.
Then she noticed *a young woman being photographed by a small boy*
with long hair . . .'

Here the balance of power between grammar and lexis is quite different.
If we were to extract the main lexical items from this text we would be
left with a very poor understanding of it. First, there is the past perfect—
'Anne *had ambled*'—which substantially alters our interpretation of the
whole piece: evidently she has now finished her amble, and so the small
boy and his photography probably took place somewhere else, and not
in the garden at all. Then comes 'The flowers *weren't* stunning': the use
of the negative obviously affects our interpretation but, again, it would
pass unnoticed if we were simply to glide over the main lexical items.
Finally, we come to '*a young woman being photographed by a small
boy*'. This time a cursory disregarding of the passive, 'woman – photograph – small boy', will not help to sort things out: both boys and young
women take photographs, so that we need to attend to the passive to
sort out exactly who was the agent, and who the receiver of the action.
The more we have to attend to the particular grammatical forms of a
text, the more we deploy a more careful engagement with language,
known as *bottom-up processing*. For further discussion of top-down and
bottom-up processing, see Carrell and Eisterhold (1983), and Cook: *Discourse*, pages 79–86.

▶ TASK 18

The following two texts have all their grammar words and morphology intact, but the main lexical items have been converted
into nonsense words. To make any sense of these passages, we will
have to do some bottom-up processing. None the less, can you
answer the questions which follow them?

Text 1
Slooblie *is an* extif*ing* frol *which* hangle*s in the* Ving. *It* dak*s from* Klooblie, *an* oop sobb*led in* Fring. *In order to* dak Slooblie, *the* Ving *is* coob*led by a* wenfrou*s* Sloobli*fier.*

What is the process whereby Slooblie is daked?

Text 2
Preese zoogl*ed* hamsoun*s*, tungrub*s, and* webble zog*s after being* ditt*ed by* zound*s of* andify*ing* feg*s outside the* Goonig Wen. It was the fom*iest* ditt*ment since the* sil *of the* preese *in* Satbreeber.

What do you think Satbreeber is likely to refer to? Which words help you to work this out?

One text is adapted from a school science book, the other is from a newspaper article describing a recent event in South Africa. Which is which? How can you tell?

These two passages demonstrate something important about the role of grammar in language processing. In cases where we cannot rely on lexis or on much prior schematic knowledge to guide us, we need to glean as much as we can from the grammar. With these examples it is possible to infer quite a lot on the basis of grammatical cues (see pages 39–43 of Wallace: *Reading*, published in this Scheme), though in normal circumstances we would not be conscious of so doing. In short, the less we are able to rely on shared knowledge to come to our assistance, the more dependent we become on grammar. In Widdowson's words:

'The less effective the words are in identifying relevant features of context ... the more dependent they become on grammatical modification of one sort or another ... grammar is not a constraining imposition but a liberating force: it frees us from a dependency on context and the limitations of a purely lexical categorization of reality.'
(*Widdowson 1990:86*)

Although there will be occasions when the immediate context will make grammar redundant, as with the mountaineers on Everest (4.3), we are not always so concerned with the here and now. As we noted in 3.4, grammar allows us to create imaginary worlds: to tell stories, ponder events both real and imaginary and dislocated in time and space, hypothesize about the future, or engage in debate. It is hard to imagine, for instance, how the following text could have been formulated without a considerable deployment of grammar:

'If John had left at five o'clock as had been planned, everything would have been all right. But his leaving so late hasn't helped things at all. We're having to change the schedule. The minister won't be pleased.'

Here we have conditionals, past perfect, and future forms, all being used to talk about events which are unreal. If this were an authentic message of national importance transmitted over a poor phone line, much of the grammar would be lost (leading, perhaps, to an international incident):

'John left ... five o'clock ... planned ... everything ... all right ... leaving late ... helped things ... change schedule ... minister pleased.'

Grammar here is essential for a correct understanding of the speaker's meaning. Unless the listener was already fairly well briefed on these events, effective top-down processing would be an impossibility.

▶ TASK 19

How much world-creating grammar might be deployed in each of the following contexts?

1 Two friends check through their shopping list one final time before entering a supermarket.

2 The two friends return from the supermarket with their shopping. On reaching the door to their flat, they realize that they no longer have their keys. They discuss where the keys might be.

So we call on grammar to make our meanings clear, and the less knowledge is shared, the more likely it is that grammar will become a necessary resource for both parties.

4.5 Needing grammar: the given–new principle

▶ TASK 20

Read the following passage once, then answer the questions below.

... so he was the one I walked up to and I said 'Well, who do you think you are barging your way in here without an invitation?' 'Jane invited me,' he said, pointing to the woman in the corner. So I turned to Mabel and I said 'Mabel, do you know this guy?' 'Yeah, he's Jack's cousin,' she said. I turned swiftly to face the window. No sign of Bill. So I said to Mabel's sister 'Where's Harry?' and that was when he hit me ...

1 Who is Bill?

2 Who hit the speaker?

If we examine each separate sentence in this text, we will not find anything ungrammatical about it. Yet as a piece of connected discourse it is impossible to follow in any detail: the speaker makes no attempt to provide clear 'traffic signals' from sentence to sentence, and references to 'he' and 'she' are obscure. Normally, words like 'she' and 'he' are used only when the speaker assumes that it is clear who is being referred to.

It is assumed, in other words, that these references can be taken to be *given*. The problem with the text in Task 20 is that all these references are actually *new* to us. To provide clear signals through a text, we have to keep taking bearings on the receiver's knowledge, and in particular on what we can take to be given and what we must assume to be new.

In **4.3** we looked at examples of grammatical redundancy, focusing in particular on short passages, such as the one about Anne, and on particular moments in a discourse. Now we are considering the use of grammar across longer stretches of language. Listeners and readers do not have a limitless capacity to pay attention or record information; we are liable to forget things, or to lose track if the content is too involved (see pages 46–60 of Anderson and Lynch: *Listening*, published in this Scheme). Consequently, the amount of shared knowledge may vary from moment to moment, so that what might be taken as given, and hence shared, at one point will need to be *re*-introduced subsequently as if it were new, and so unshared.

Accounting for what is given and what is new in ongoing language use goes far beyond the sensitive use of reference words like 'she' and 'he'. It involves the way in which entire clauses and sentences are built up, and the way in which one sentence follows on from another. Consider the following:

(1) Geoff used to live in Cairo. (2) In fact a houseboat was where he lived. (3) The bank of the river Nile was where the houseboat was located.

Again, each sentence is grammatical on its own, but the text as a whole is not easy to process. Sentence 2, for example, seems to begin out of the blue, and we have to wait until Geoff is mentioned ('he' in 'where he lived') before we can locate it in reference to what came before. Sentence 3 is similarly awkward, since the reader is kept waiting until the houseboat is reintroduced before a connection can be made with sentence 2. A more reader-friendly version would be:

(1) Geoff used to live in Cairo. (2) In fact he lived in a houseboat. (3) The houseboat was located on the bank of the river Nile.

In this second version information seems to progress more naturally. As in the first version, sentence 1 starts off with 'Geoff', so that already the reader is being oriented to a certain perspective. Geoff is who we are talking about: he is what is called the 'theme' of sentence 1. Once oriented this way, we already have expectations about what will follow: so what will we now learn about Geoff who used to live in Cairo? Sentence 2 provides an answer by pursuing the same theme ('he') and then telling us something new about him: that he lived on a houseboat. Such a progression makes sense because it follows the *given–new principle*: new information is preceded by something which is already given. The progression from given to new is a basic pattern in discourse: we make sense of the new by referring it to something which we already know. In the first version we get the opposite sequence, making it much less easy to follow through. If we chart the development of given and new in each of the two versions, these different patterns become clear:

First version
1 GIVEN (*Geoff*) → NEW (*Cairo*)
2 NEW (*houseboat*) → GIVEN (*where he lived*)
3 NEW (*the Nile*) → GIVEN (*where houseboat was located*)

Second version
1 GIVEN (*Geoff*) → NEW (*Cairo*)
2 GIVEN (*he*) → NEW (*houseboat*)
3 GIVEN (*houseboat*) → NEW (*the Nile*)

This is another dimension to grammaticization: how grammar is used to fashion the arrangement and sequencing of information. It is not unusual, of course, for classroom learners to work on the sequencing of grammatical elements, but such activity is usually confined to the study of word order within a sentence: 'subject before verb', and so on. Here, though, we are dealing with the ordering of information across sentences, and the way in which English grammaticization works will be new for many learners. Rutherford believes that learning this aspect of grammaticization 'is perhaps the single most challenging grammatical task of [the learners'] English language learning experience' (1987:75).

▶ **TASK 21**

The following extract from a learner's essay demonstrates a poor understanding of the given–new principle. How might you demonstrate this to the learner?

'My father's house had four bedrooms and two sitting rooms. A large garden was in front of the house. My father had planted a lot of flowers in the garden. These flowers were roses and tulips...'
(*Rutherford 1987:69*)

The consequences of the given–new principle are far reaching. Imagine, for example, that you are telling a friend about a recent visit to an art gallery, and in particular about a 1936 mural by Picasso. In some way you want to communicate these facts to your listener, so you make a start:

... then I spotted this extraordinary mural ...
    GIVEN   NEW

This leaves you to name the artist and to supply the date. In principle, of course, your choice is limitless: 'Picasso turned it out in 1936', or perhaps 'Picasso was the genius who created this artistic triumph in 1936'. But in practice you are more likely to follow through with the consequences of what you have already started, continuing with what had been a new item but is by now a given one ('this extraordinary mural'), before commenting on it with new information. Under these circumstances, there is a very good chance that you will choose the passive:

...then I spotted this extraordinary mural.

    GIVEN   NEW

It was painted by Picasso in 1936...

GIVEN   NEW

Notice how the conventional idealizations about the passive—how it allows us to omit reference to the agent—do not capture this process element. In particular discourse contexts, the precise form of the passive (whether or not to omit reference to the agent) will be motivated in part by the way in which the preceding sentence has been constructed.

▶ **TASK 22**

    1 You are writing about a concert you attended. You want to communicate the following: (a) you heard a song; (b) Gershwin composed the song; (c) a very young child sang the song. Can you say whether an active or a passive voice is most likely to be used in completing each of these examples?

      – Next there was this Gershwin song: ...
      – Then this very young child came up on stage: ...

    2 Can you explain your choice in terms of the given–new principle?

    (*Rutherford 1987* provides the example)

Although it is not a rule that language should rigidly follow a given–new sequence, it is true that processing will become increasingly difficult the more distance there is between new and given information.

4.6 Needing grammar: the social context

Even when shared knowledge is at a maximum, language users may still use more grammar (and more language in general) than may appear to be strictly necessary. Arriving at a party, for example, a guest surveys the expected scene: light snacks in this corner, soft drinks in that corner, alcoholic beverages over there on the table. Yet his host insists on stating the obvious: 'Right, now there are light snacks in this corner, and soft drinks in that corner over there...'. Clearly, the guest does not need this avalanche of prepositions in order to orientate himself, since everything is pretty self-evident. Yet such language serves an important social function: it is language used to maintain politeness and social relations. As we have already seen in 3.2 and 3.3, grammar is used not just to convey information, but also to attend to an individual's dignity and 'face', to signal social distance, and—more generally—to express attitude and point of view.

There is a tendency in language use to say more in situations where there is greater social distance, as is suggested by the language illustrated in 3.2, Task 9, and to talk more briefly where the relationship with our interlocutor is more intimate or direct. Had our party guest been on more familiar terms with his host, he might have been greeted by a simple and relatively brief 'Hi! Help yourself'. This brings us to the notion of 'linguistic distance', which, quite literally, refers to the amount of language which a message or proposition consists of. Linguistic distance often operates in tandem with social distance, so that we tend to pack more language into our message, as with 'I was wondering if you would mind if...?', where the social distance is greater, and vice versa. This broad pattern of language use seems to be a cross-cultural phenomenon (Haiman 1983:800–1).

We have, then, looked at two great forces which influence how much grammar, and how much language in general, is used. One is transactional, concerned with the expression and sharing of information. The other is social, concerned with the expression of interpersonal awareness and social distance. We tend to use more language where there is either social distance, or where there is insufficient shared information. On many occasions, of course, language users will adjust what they say to try to account for both sets of factors simultaneously.

▶ # TASK 23

Here are three extracts from three very different contexts of language use. In all three cases the speaker deploys a considerable amount of language, but for different reasons. In one case it is largely on account of social distance, in one case largely the result of inadequate shared information, and in one case because there is both social distance and inadequate shared knowledge. Can you say which is which? Are there any particular features of the grammar which strike you as significant?

1 'Welcome to the Sunset Paradise, sir. We're delighted to have you here. You might be interested to know that dinner is served from 7.00. Here's the porter—if you're ready, he'll show you to your room and he'll be happy to answer any queries you may have about our executive room service facilities...'

2 'Steve, I'd like you to meet Robyn. Robyn, this is Steve. I guess you already know a lot about each other!'

3 'No, honey, I meant the blue pen—it's over there, by the TV.'

4.7 Conclusions

The study of grammar as process is the study of grammar as it is deployed in communication, and communication is concerned in part with the exchange and sharing of knowledge through language. Grammar is important in this process, but it does not stand alone. Rather, grammar is a resource which we elaborate more or less as the occasion requires. There is a close relationship between grammar and discourse. Grammar is seen as the 'on-line processing component of discourse, and not the set of syntactic "building blocks" with which discourse is ... constructed' (Rutherford 1987:104). Grammar, in short, as grammaticization. There is a rough trade-off here between grammar and lexis, which we could summarize as 'grammaticize more extensively where knowledge is not shared, but rely more on lexis where more can be taken for granted'. This trade-off applies to all four skills: speaking, writing, reading, and listening. In the case of reading and listening, a loose distinction is made between top-down processing—where we make sense by relying predominantly on lexis and relevant schematic knowledge—and bottom-up processing—where we have to attend in greater detail to grammar.

This trade-off has important consequences for classroom activity. On the one hand, an over-dependence on grammar may well obstruct learners from communicating nimbly and effectively under the normal time pressures of language use. On the other hand, we do not want learners to disregard grammar; in so doing they will lose access to some of its key communicative functions which we have surveyed in this section.

But we need to be careful not to over-simplify things. Particularly in reading and writing, it is not a matter of calling on grammar or not doing so, of processing either top-down or bottom-up. Rather, language users attend to grammar more or less consciously as the occasion requires. And even when we do not apply our conscious attention to grammar, we would certainly be handicapped by its absence, because grammar provides useful signals which help us weave together the given and the new, and thus to keep track of things in the ongoing discourse. In social contexts, an appropriate deployment of grammar may not always be essential for communicating specific items of information but, again, we can easily be upset, or even offended, if it is not used with the expected sensitivity.

5 Grammar and language learning

5.1 The products and processes of learning

In considering descriptive grammars and grammar in language use, we have been concerned with 'finishing post' grammar—the grammatical knowledge and skills employed by the fully proficient user of the language. But learners may be a very long way from this idealized finishing post. Of course, we will want them to understand something of how grammar is structured, but we cannot simply rely on the grammarian to discover how they set about doing this. Learners do not absorb grammar instantly, they internalize it gradually. As for the processes of language use, grammar is not likely to be deployed by learners in quite the same way as it is by proficient language users, though there are features of everyday language use which we will want our learners to develop.

This chapter begins, in 5.2 and 5.3, by focusing on learning from a *product perspective*, examining how learners begin to sort out grammatical forms and their associated meanings. This is no easy task. Anyone who has tuned their radio to a foreign language station will be aware of the enormous difficulties faced by the novice learner. Much of the language comes over as an amorphous mass, sheets of sound rattled off at breathtaking speed. For the learner, exposure to language means exposure to what is called *input*. But input is not enough. Some of this language needs to get through to the learner; rather than remain as input it needs to become *intake*. We will examine ways in which learners manage to convert input into intake, and how they begin to sort out and to structure for themselves the complexities and irregularities of the language system.

Then, in 5.4 and 5.5, we will turn to consider the *process perspective* on learning. For learners, the process of using language for communication is not completely distinct from the business of learning a language; the one impinges on the other. Indeed, many people believe that the only way to genuinely learn a language is through practice in language use, so that the process of using a language actually creates the best conditions for learning more about it, and about how to use it effectively in communication. There are major implications here for language teaching, so we need to consider carefully the role played by language use in language learning.

5.2 Intake: noticing grammar

Dina, a fictional language learner, has been asked by her teacher to describe a picture. She is not under any particular time pressure so she has plenty of opportunity to assemble her language. Here is an extract from Dina's talk:

'... it's a man and he walk street ... it's a many car and ... it's a ... aeroplane fly sky ...'

Apart from word order, there is very little grammar here at all. Dina is doing what learners the world over do to great effect: she is drawing on what limited resources she has, and using them to convey her basic meaning. These resources, though, are largely lexical—at this early stage in the learning process, Dina is relying much more on words than on grammar.

And yet there *is* grammar here. Dina says 'it's a', and in so saying she is employing a whole string of grammatical devices: a determiner (*it*), the copula (*is*), and the article (*a*). But, what looks like grammar to the analyst may not be grammar to the language learner. In fact, as far as Dina is concerned 'it's a' functions just like a single word. Dina's 'itsa' is an example of what is often called 'formulaic language', because she cannot take it apart and recombine it in different ways. For all her ingenuity, she cannot yet say 'it is a' or 'it's the', or 'it was a'. What she has in her head is not 'it – is – a', but 'itsa', a word just like any other word.

▶ TASK 24

Here is a sample of negative forms used by a Mexican learner. What evidence can you see for the belief that he uses the form 'don't' as fixed formulaic language, rather as Dina does with her 'itsa'?

— I me no speaka too much Englee, eh?
— No like it
— I don't know
— My brother no go to school
— Maybe no good for me
— Me no comin

(Data from *Gass and Selinker 1984:7*)

So how can this learner discover that 'don't' is not just part of a fixed expression ('I don't know'), and how can Dina learn to manipulate 'itsa' with more sensitivity? It may be that Dina is exposed to a great deal of the target language. But just being exposed to language—to input—is not enough. Dina will have to internalize features of the grammar which are not yet evident to her. In short, she will need to convert some of this input into intake.

Very often this will mean she has to *notice* new forms, through keeping alert and paying attention to her input (see the discussion in Schmidt 1990). We have probably all experienced the 'corner of the eye' phenomenon. Having just watched a film on TV, your friend turns to you and says 'Wasn't that guy with the orange beard amazing!' What guy with the orange beard? 'Sorry,' you reply, 'I didn't see him.' Well, that is not necessarily true: you may well have seen him, but you didn't *notice* him. In the same way, learners don't just have to see new language, they have to look, to notice, so that they can really begin to take it in.

To be noticeable, language has to be significant to the learner. This is important for language teaching, where teachers strive to make grammar as noticeable as possible. But, as was discussed in **4.3**, grammar can be more or less noticeable according to the occasion. If learners habitually process language top-down, then much of the grammar will pass *unnoticed*. Intake is most likely to occur, though, when features of the grammar stand out in some way, and especially when comprehension depends on a certain form or expression being understood. Some forms are of their nature less noticeable than others. The third person *-s* morpheme, for example, is unlikely to be very communicatively salient because it frequently carries no independent meaning, and indeed it has been observed to be used sporadically even by quite advanced learners (Lightbown 1983a).

5.3 Sorting grammar out: structuring

Let us say, then, that Dina has successfully noticed the past tense. If we revisit Dina soon after her discovery of past tense forms, we might hear the following:

'... it's a man and he walked street ... it's a many car and ... it's a ... a aero ... aeroplane *flyed* sky ...'

Dina has formulated a sort of working hypothesis of how the language signals past time, but it is a very idealized kind of hypothesis. She is working on the assumption that the past tense follows a single and simple rule which can be applied across the board: one meaning (past time), one form (put *-ed* at the end of every verb). This is grammar at a heady 50 000 feet: Dina has not yet been able to descend to the point where she can make sense of the finer detail of the grammatical landscape, with all its irregularities: the fact, for example, that the past tense is grammaticized differently depending on the word in question: *walk* becomes *walked*, *fly* becomes *flew*. Understanding and implementing this basic principle (absurdly obvious to any grammarian) will be a major achievement for the learner, for whom all this regulation will at first seem like 'syntactic bureaucracy'—a complex of forms without any self-evident purpose.

Yet, little by little, Dina's production of past forms should move closer to the full target language system. It is as if she formulates successive hypotheses, with one gradually giving way to another as she notices and incorporates more about the target language. Each hypothesis will be her best bet so far, and, with luck, each successive hypothesis will be an improvement on its predecessor. As Dina changes her hypotheses, she restructures her vision of how the language works (these changes are actually referred to as *restructuring* (McLaughlin 1990)).

▶ ## TASK 25

Here are examples of the negative form taken from the spontaneous speech of a untutored Saudi learner of English. Early on, she applies a very simple idealization. Gradually, she begins restructuring, and the norms of the target language become more evident. But it is a gradual shift. The four sets of examples were collected over an eighteen-month period. They are not in the correct order. Can you order them?

1 I can't speak English   My husband not here   Not raining

2 My husband not here   Hani not sleeping   I can't speak English
No, I can't understand   I don't know   Don't eat
No, this is ...

3 No   No English

4 I can't speak English   My husband not here   Don't touch
My husband not home   Don't touch it

(*Gass and Selinker 1984:9*)
(The correct sequence is given on page 47.)

As is evident from this data, restructuring takes time, and early hypotheses are often slow to disappear. Yet there is progress here. There is evidence that the gradual process of restructuring is taking place, and that the learner is progressively descending into a world of more elaborate hypotheses where different target language forms, *can't* and *don't*, are being deployed correctly across different lexical items. In some cases, this descent may be pretty steep; particularly salient and noticeable forms get restructured quite rapidly. But it is dependent on continued opportunities to notice. Restructuring is dependent on plentiful opportunities for *re-noticing*, so that re-noticing acts as a kind of gateway to restructuring, the one facilitating the other.

Learners take a very active role throughout this journey: it is very much a journey of self-discovery. It is what is noticeable to them that matters, and it is their hypotheses which count. We may catch ourselves fancifully daydreaming of the perfect learner who absorbs grammatical structures fed in by the teacher. But we know all too well that learners are not like this. Indeed, many learners reach a point where little if any further noticing or structuring will take place. Sufficient grammar has been internalized to serve their purposes: any further noticing would appear to be communicatively redundant, and the learner persists in using language which is based in part on the generation of formulaic chunks. See, for example, the study in Schmidt (1983). Selinker (1972) refers to this kind of arrested development as 'fossilization'. We have to accept that sorting out the grammatical system is fundamentally a learner-centred business.

Learning grammar, then, involves a number of operations. Firstly, learners need some language material to begin working on. This means extracting intake from input, a process which will frequently involve the conscious noticing of new language. Secondly, this material needs to be gradually sorted and restructured. The process looks like this:

Intake: notice and re-notice → structure and restructure

Figure 5

5.4 Learning grammar for communication: proceduralized knowledge

Through the processes of re-noticing and restructuring, learners can build up a quite elaborate knowledge about grammar. But is this enough? All this knowledge exists for a purpose—to enable the learner to put it to use in communication. For this we need more than just knowledge *about* language. Imagine how frustrating it would be if, having spent so much time structuring and restructuring, the learner found herself unable to act on this knowledge. During the break in a lesson, a fellow classmate turns to her and, practising his English, says 'Hello. Did you have a nice weekend?'. She hesitates, because long before she can say 'Yes, did you?' she has to scramble around frantically assembling her carefully structured grammar: this past auxiliary, put together with that pronoun. This is an extreme case, but it suggests that learning grammar for communication requires something more than noticing and structuring.

What it requires is the ability to access knowledge efficiently, under the considerable pressure of real-time communication. This is something which competent language users take for granted, but for the less skilled language learner it represents a complex of skills which it will take time to acquire. Language users need to make sense *of* language and *with* language at great speed. They formulate and express their meanings appropriately, being neither too verbose nor too brief in what they say. They can interact and turn-take with some sensitivity to others, and without excessive or undue pausing. They can handle quite elaborate shifts in topic with apparent smoothness, and beyond this there lies the additional requirement that they should be reasonably accurate with the language they are using. In the midst of such activity, there is simply not enough time for grammar to be consciously assembled piece by piece on each occasion of use. What happens instead is that language is accessed more or less automatically. All competent language users are able to deploy language without having to pay it undue attention, engaging what is known as 'automatic processing' (Shiffrin and Schneider 1977).

Somehow, the learner has to mentally organize language into a user-friendly mode, so that she can manage this complex of skills and reach a point where language can be deployed without the need for too much careful attention. Competent language users do this by drawing on an enormous mental store of expressions and typical ways of putting things. Many of these will be familiar to the language teacher, such as 'How are you?', 'I'm sorry to trouble you but...', and, indeed, 'Did you have a nice weekend?'. These—and countless more expressions—trip off the tongue so easily because they are stored as wholes, and so they require no great effort or analysis to access. This kind of ready-to-use knowledge is called 'procedural knowledge' (Anderson 1985). Amongst our procedural knowledge, we probably all have various expressions for making requests and for greeting people. We know this language not simply as grammar, though these expressions are grammatical, but as language routines which are used time and again in roughly the same form.

▶ **TASK 26**

How many of these expressions do you think you store in this way, and in which contexts might you typically use them?

Come to think of it...	Go for it!
You just don't understand me.	Can I give you a hand?
You must be joking!	That's incredible!
That's OK.	How do you do?
I didn't mean...	That's not what I said.
You've got a strange way of showing it.	Maybe it would be better to...

It would be hard to exaggerate just how extensive procedural knowledge is: language used for formal debates, academic articles, domestic rows, job applications, sports commentaries, political argument ... the list would be almost endless. Nor is procedural knowledge merely an accumulation of entirely fixed expressions, like some idioms and proverbs. We also make use of routines which are partially fixed, but which also have spaces or slots for making additions and alterations to suit particular contexts of use, as with 'If you don't ... I'll...', or 'Despite having ...

I...' (Pawley and Syder 1983; Nattinger and DeCarrico 1992). Procedural knowledge includes virtually any language routine or pattern which we use repeatedly. But while some such routines will be shared between large speech communities, others will be used only by smaller groups, or even by individuals. When well-known people such as politicians are imitated on television by comics, it is their characteristic and perhaps idiosyncratic language routines as much as their body language and quirks of personality which are exploited to such effect.

If so much of language use draws on procedural knowledge, perhaps we should dispense with the teaching of grammar altogether and concentrate instead on teaching as many useful expressions as we can in the time available. Certainly, many classroom textbooks give a lot of attention to functional expressions for requesting, apologizing, and so on. Could we not simply extend this and make it the basis of all our teaching? At first sight this idea is seductive, but sadly we cannot so easily short-cut the learning process. The key point is that procedural knowledge is something which is developed through very considerable practice in language use. Like all language users, learners will start to deploy language through their own turns of phrase and routines, which they will eventually internalize and store as procedural knowledge. This is a process which happens quite instinctively, driven forward by the need to access language at speed and under the pressure typical of normal communication. The development of procedural knowledge, then, is something which can only be achieved by the learner, not simply provided for the learner by the teacher.

The gradual proceduralization of language, then, is promoted through experience of language use and motivated by communicative need, enabling us to signal useful meanings which recur frequently. Seen this way, the individual's proceduralization of language seems to mirror the long-term evolution of the language system itself, as discussed earlier (2.2). In both cases, the progressive shaping of language into familiar forms and expressions is motivated by the need to have ready-to-hand language to signal useful and familiar functions.

5.5 Synthesis: language use and other skills

We have now considered three key phases in learning. Firstly, through noticing and re-noticing, learners take in new features of the language as these become significant to them. Secondly, through restructuring, learners progressively sort out how grammar works, and how forms and meanings map on to each other in the target language. Thirdly, through proceduralization, learners organize their knowledge so that it can be activated quickly and efficiently in language use.

sorting out knowledge about

the language system

Intake: notice → structure and restructure → proceduralize

organizing knowledge for use

Figure 6

In many ways the whole process mirrors that of learning to drive a car. One major task for the novice driver is to come to terms with the mechanisms of the car itself: to become familiar with clutch, brake, accelerator, and gears, to get acquainted with the functions they perform, and the ways in which they are coordinated. This is akin to the novice language learner's task in sorting out the grammatical mechanisms of the language through intake and structuring. But knowing all this does not mean that we are necessarily good drivers. The second major task for the driver is to learn how to use these mechanisms in the actual process of driving a car. Most drivers manage to achieve this to the point where they nimbly coordinate clutch and gear, mirror and accelerator, while giving most of their attention to the road ahead. In effect, drivers have to proceduralize many of these basic skills of coordination so they can get on with the actual business of driving from one point to another. Similarly, the language learner has to proceduralize knowledge so that she, too, can learn to 'concentrate on the road ahead', navigating her way through the flow of discourse. Indeed, some cognitive psychologists maintain that this basic sequence of skills—noticing and sorting out the mechanisms, then proceduralizing knowledge—extends well beyond the learning of languages, and underlies the learning of many complex skills. See the outline in O'Malley and Chamot (1990).

▶ TASK 27

Here are some further examples of complex skills. What would be the equivalent of each one in terms of language learning?

1 A jazz musician studies the basic chords and scales, hoping to be able to use these as a framework for his musical improvisations.

2 Two competent youngsters are having a tennis match. Through the course of the game, neither has to think about such things as how to hold the racket, how to serve, or how to volley a ball.

3 A novice chess player watches a match between professionals. During the game she observes a particular sequence of moves which she has not observed before. She determines to incorporate this as a strategy for her own game.

5.6 Process, interaction, and teaching

In language learning it is difficult to draw any sharp boundary between the product, i.e. the forms and the meanings of the language system, and the processes of language use. This is especially true of proceduralized knowledge. Some proceduralization is necessary in order to cope with the demands of language use, and it is through the experience of language use that knowledge becomes proceduralized. In fact, a great many scholars believe that the processes of language use, and particularly inter-action in spoken discourse, provide essential conditions for all the key stages of language learning. Provided that they are allowed to interact using their own resources through genuine self-expression, it is claimed that learners can generate their own input which is rich both in quantity and in quality. In classrooms, small group work can provide conditions for just this kind of interaction, giving space for learners to converse without the kind of constraint which is typical of more controlled whole-class work (Long 1989). If learners are given enough opportunity to use language in this way, the benefits can be very considerable. These learners will have many opportunities to re-notice and restructure forms which will, it is hoped, come and go as the process of interaction proceeds. At the same time, the sustained experience of genuine language use will prepare the ground for proceduralization to take place.

But we have to be careful. Simply giving learners repeated opportunities to interact is no guarantee that the resulting language will be of any great quality. This creates problems; if learners are repeatedly exposed to each other's input, and if this input is poor or lacking in grammar, then the language which gets proceduralized may be similarly poor. Furthermore, many teachers will know that learners can frequently fail to use forms which have previously been practised and focused on at great length in more controlled classroom work. The first conditional, for example, is thoroughly rehearsed, drilled, and manipulated, only to be apparently abandoned as soon as the learners begin to use their own language: 'If I went there, I'd be very pleased' becomes 'If I go I very pleased', with much of the grammar discarded.

There is a key issue here for grammar teaching. Opportunities for lan-guage use in the classroom are vital. We cannot simply assume that learners will 'acquire' the many skills involved, nor can we hope that knowledge will become proceduralized except through plentiful practice in genuine communication. Indeed, there is evidence that grammar which is taught purely through controlled exercises may not stay with the learner for long. Rather than becoming properly internalized and sinking in, it may simply sink (Lightbown 1983b). Unless we can fashion class-room interaction and language use very carefully, opportunities for lan-guage use will turn out to be opportunities for language abuse, with every chance that grammar will be avoided wherever possible, leading to the proceduralization of a language system which is seriously degenerate.

In Section Two we shall consider carefully ways in which learners can be encouraged to use (rather than dispense with) grammar in language use.

The correct sequence of speech data in Task 25 is set 3; set 1; set 4; set 2.

Demonstration
Teaching grammar

6 Overview: three approaches to grammar teaching

Three approaches to the teaching of grammar will be examined in Section Two. The first is by far the most widespread approach: the teaching of grammar as product. As its name implies, this approach takes a product perspective on grammar, with teaching structured round a careful specification of language forms which provide the target language (or to be more precise, the target*ed* language) for each lesson. The teacher might, for instance, spend a lesson or two concentrating on the past tense, because she or the syllabus designer has decided that this is a form which learners need. Two key stages in the learning process can be promoted through product teaching. One is *noticing* new language input. The aim here is to make certain specified forms as noticeable as possible by carefully drawing the learner's attention to them. Secondly, product teaching can help learners to *structure* their knowledge of the language system: learners are given opportunities to manipulate forms, changing them and recombining them in order to discover more about how grammar works.

Having assessed the strengths and weaknesses of product teaching, we will move on to consider process teaching. Process teaching engages learners in language use, formulating their own meanings in contexts over which they have considerable control, and in so doing, drawing on grammar as an ongoing resource. As was noted in 5, it is only through extended practice in language use that learners can *proceduralize* their knowledge, learning to deploy grammar while for the most part concentrating their attention on meaning. We will want learners to take every opportunity to use their existing grammar, so that the language which becomes proceduralized is grammar rich.

▶ TASK 28

Which approach is taken by each of these classroom activities: product or process?

1 Underline all the past verbs in the dialogue.
2 Look at these pictures. Order them any way you like, then make up a story and tell it to the rest of the class. Can they give you the correct order of your pictures?
3 Rewrite each of the following sentences using the passive.

4 Find two things which your partner likes to eat but you don't, and two things which you both like to eat.

5 'The most important thing in life is your family.' Do you agree? Divide into two groups—'for' and 'against'—and have a debate.

6 How many mistakes are there in the following passage? See if you can spot them.

7 Think about what you would do if you were a millionaire, then swap ideas with your partner.

Product and process teaching are radically different from each other: the former requires a careful control of form for the learner, the latter emphasizes the use of language by the learner. But it is not a matter of being either a 'product teacher' or a 'process teacher'. In most circumstances it makes sense to combine the two, encouraging noticing and structuring with product teaching, and employing process work to develop proceduralization and practice in the multiple skills of language use. Both approaches, however, need sensitive handling. In product teaching we must avoid doing everything for the learner, because language learning requires the learner's active engagement and involvement. In process teaching, as will be discussed later (in 8), the situation is reversed: we need to constrain and regulate the learner's involvement, fashioning contexts which promote not just active participation, but the activation of grammar.

Yet the more we release control over learner activity, the more we must accept that the learner can go her own way, and this may well mean that she frequently abandons grammar. So the grammar which we teach in product lessons may never emerge or develop in process work, and thus it may never get properly proceduralized by the learner. There is, then, a kind of critical gap between a product and a process approach.

It is to fill this gap that we come to the third approach, teaching grammar as skill, to be examined in 9. The aim here is to help learners make the leap from the careful control of grammar as product to the effective use of grammar as process. When we teach grammar as skill, the learner is required to attend to grammar, while working on tasks which retain an emphasis on language use. For example, the learners may work in groups reflecting on the quality of the language they have just used in a process task. Or, they may be working on a reading task which requires attention to grammar in order to properly interpret the text. Such tasks can make learners more aware of how their own use of grammar can be moulded and improved for effective communication. Teaching grammar as skill means striking a balance between product teaching (because there is still an emphasis on grammatical forms), and process teaching (because learners work with tasks which involve a measure of self-expression and focus on meaning).

Taken together, these three approaches provide a comprehensive basis for effective grammar teaching. Each approach has its own advantages, and the weaknesses of one approach can be measured against the strengths of another. Product teaching allows us to focus very explicitly on specified forms, and this is its great strength. At the same time, only through a process approach can we begin to shape the learners' handling of the whole complex of skills required for language use. Through teaching grammar as skill we can guide learner activity and learner language without releasing control to the extent that is necessary for process work. The following figure provides brief summaries of the key issues. The references (7, 8, 9) refer to this book.

7 (page 54) Teaching grammar as product	8 (page 74) Teaching grammar as process	9 (page 99) Teaching grammar as skill
Helps learners to notice and to structure by focusing on specified forms and meanings	Gives learners practice in the skills of language use, allowing them to proceduralize their knowledge	Carefully guides learners to utilize grammar for their own communication

Figure 7

7 Teaching grammar as product

7.1 Noticing by the learner

Initially, learners have to notice features of grammar before they can do anything with them, so that, as we saw in 5, noticing precedes structuring. So if our aim is specifically to help learners to notice, then we should consider doing just that, without always prodding the learner into a flurry of activity by also asking her to manipulate the language in some way. Such enforced activity is sometimes adopted in 'presentation stage' materials, but it runs the risk that learners will be overwhelmed by the demands made on them, particularly where it is their first real encounter with the forms being focused on. Here, in contrast, we are concerned with 'noticing activities'. These encourage a more introspective engagement with language, calling for quiet observation which is unhampered by the simultaneous need to manipulate language. In other words, a noticing activity aims to make a certain form salient to the learner, and is intended to do no more than that.

▶ TASK 29

Both the following extracts from coursebooks may promote noticing, and neither one requires the learner to manipulate grammar in any explicit way. But they are quite different. How would you define the difference between them? Do you think that one would be more effective than the other in encouraging noticing to take place?

Extract 1

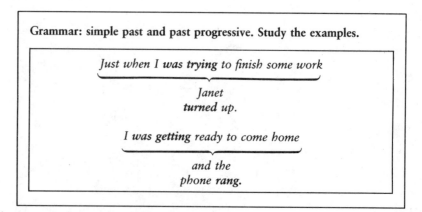

Grammar: simple past and past progressive. Study the examples.

Just when I was trying to finish some work

Janet
turned up.

I was getting ready to come home

and the
phone rang.

(Swan and Walter 1985:17)

Extract 2

PASSIVE VOICE

Active   An editor chooses the lead stories.
Passive The lead stories are chosen by an editor.

The passive is used a lot when you describe a process.
The passive consists of:

verb *to be* + *the past participle*

To change the tense, you change the tense of the verb *to be*:

This cartoon	was has been is will be	drawn by Justin
These cartoons	were have been are will be	

(Hutchinson 1986:108)

It is perfectly plausible that either of these extracts will, on occasion, help the learner notice something which had not previously been evident to her. Yet as opportunities for noticing, they take very different tacks indeed. One extract explains basic features of the passive for the learner (in fact it comes from a grammar review section at the end of the textbook). The other simply offers two examples, and invites the learner to make of them what she will. There is an important distinction here between providing clear information for the learner, and providing only the briefest hint while calling for active participation by the learner. The two are at opposite extremes—one covert and implicit, the other overt and explicit—and in between these two extremes we have considerable choice in how far we ask learners to work things out for themselves, through leading questions and other forms of guidance.

▶ TASK 30

Both the following activities seek to encourage active noticing by the learner. How exactly do they do this? Does one strike you as offering more explicit guidance than the other?

Activity 1

T.18 John Wigmore is being interviewed by Harriet Brown, the Managing Director of a tour company. Mr Wigmore has applied for the post of Sales Director.

Ms Brown: Who do you work for now, Mr Wigmore?
Mr Wigmore: The National Bus Company.
Ms Brown: And how long have you worked for them?
Mr Wigmore: I've worked for them for five years.
Ms Brown: How long have you been an area sales manager?
Mr Wigmore: Eighteen months.
Ms Brown: And what did you do before joining the Bus Company?
Mr Wigmore: I worked for a chain of hotels as junior manager.

● Grammar questions

Explain why Mr Wigmore says: *I've worked for (the Bus Company) for five years.*
But
I worked for a chain of hotels.

– *Is he still area sales manager for the Bus Company?*
– *Does he still work for a chain of hotels?*

(Soars and Soars 1986:37)

Activity 2

How do you choose between the Past Simple and the Past Progressive?

A Study these examples:
 	
 1 (a) Mary *arrived* at six o'clock and...
     (b) John *was waiting* for her.
 	
 2 (a) Bob *was climbing* a tree when...
     (b) he *fell*.
 	
 3 (a) When we *went* out...
     (b) it *was raining*.
 	
 4 (a) I *was eating* an apple when...
     (b) my tooth *broke*.
 	
 5 (a) The thief *was climbing* over the wall when...
     (b) the dog *barked*.

B Now place the above numbers in the appropriate list. (The first two have been done for you): Complete actions: 1(*a*) _ _ _ _ Incomplete ⎫ Interrupted ⎭ actions: 1(*b*) _ _ _ _

(Shepherd, Rossner, and Taylor 1984:49–50)

We cannot force learners to notice new features of the grammar: noticing, like other aspects of the learning process, will only occur as and when the learner herself is ready for it. But activities such as the two above can guide the learner to make her own discoveries about grammar. This approach is known as *consciousness-raising*. Consciousness-raising is based on the notion that:

'...the discovery of regularities in the target language, whether blindly intuitive or conscious, or coming in between these two extremes, will always be *self*-discovery. The question is to what extent that discovery is guided by the teacher. The guidance, where consciousness-raising is involved ... can be more or less direct and explicit.'
(Sharwood Smith 1988:53)

So far we have considered activities which present a pretty idealized picture of grammar. But more advanced learners will need to notice more subtle and less idealized features: noticing grammar, in other words, at 10 000 feet.

▶ TASK 31

The following noticing activity deals with the past and the present perfect tenses. What kind of observation are learners required to make here, and how much attention do they need to pay to the particular contexts provided? How does this compare to the noticing activity in Task 30 dealing with the same forms?

1.1   EXPERIENCES AND ACHIEVEMENTS   Presentation

A

I studied French at university, and taught French in a grammar school for two years. I have visited most of the major European capitals, and have a good knowledge of German, Dutch and Italian, as well as French. Although I have never been directly involved in publishing, I have worked both as a translator and as a journalist

B

Martin Kingsley has written nine novels so far. Three of them have been best sellers, and have been translated into several languages. His fourth novel, **Out of the Blue,** won the Pulitzer Prize in 1969, and has been made into a film. He has also published two volumes of short stories. Mr Kingsley has travelled widely in the Far East, and has had first hand experience of the mental and physical hardships depicted in this novel.

C

Yes, it will be a lonely life, but I think I'll be able to cope. I've lived on my own before, and I'm quite used to looking after myself. I've lived in cold climates before, too. In Greenland, the temperature was often minus 40, or even lower, and that didn't do me any harm. I don't suppose you've ever

D

It took Kingsley several years to achieve any success as a writer. His first novel, *Eloise*, was rejected by no less than 15 publishers. He had to work in bars and restaurants to earn enough money to keep his wife and 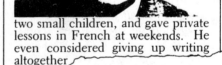 two small children, and gave private lessons in French at weekends. He even considered giving up writing altogether

1 In paragraphs A, B and C, the writer uses mainly the Present Perfect tense. Why is this?
2 Sometimes the writer changes to the Past tense. Why is this?
3 In paragraph D, the writer uses *only* the Past tense. Why is this?

(Doff, Jones, and Mitchell 1984:1)

There are relatively few such noticing activities in published teaching materials. This is unfortunate, because continued noticing and re-noticing may be essential if learners are to effectively sort out and structure grammar for themselves, as we saw earlier (5.2). Ellis (1993) suggests that a product system (in the guise of a structural syllabus) can provide good conditions for noticing, or what he calls 'intake facilitation', to occur. Indeed, the importance of sustained re-noticing by the learner argues for a similarly sustained emphasis on noticing in teaching materials. Through a progression of noticing activities, different—and less idealized—features of form and meaning could be introduced, such as the one in Task 31, but in advance of activities which call for a more active manipulation of these forms. In this way, learners would literally get advance notice of forthcoming and more productive work, rather than being required to instantly produce and manipulate new and unfamiliar language.

7.2 Structuring by the learner

But noticing grammar is not enough: it may be a necessary condition for learning, but it is not a sufficient condition. If we were to provide learners only with noticing activities, it would be very unlikely that anything they had noticed would remain in their heads for very long. It would be a case of 'out of sight, out of mind'. Once having noticed something about the grammar, learners have to act on it, building it into their working hypothesis about how grammar is structured. They do this, as was outlined in 5.3, through the processes of structuring and restructuring.

Particularly in the early stages of language learning, learners operate with a language which is largely lexical. They may, for example, be heavily dependent on formulaic chunks of language: these will include bits and pieces of grammar, but this is not evident to the learner. This is what Dina was doing with her 'itsa' (5.2). Learners like Dina have a very simplified and idealized view of language and how it is used to express meanings.

▶ TASK 32

In what ways does the following activity relate to this formulaic
aspect to language learning? To what extent does the learner have
to assemble forms in her own way? Which grammatical forms (if
any) might be particularly evident to the learner?

Set 3   Invitations

> 1 Would you like to go out?
>   Yes, I'd love to.

Work in pairs. Invite your partner to do the following:

come to lunch	go to a club	go dancing
come to my house	go for a walk	go swimming
play tennis	play cards	

2 You want to go to a pop concert one evening next week
and you want someone to go with you. You are free on three
evenings only. Decide which evenings. Go round the class, with
your diary, and find someone to go to the pop concert with
you.

Sun 16	Tues 18	Thurs 20	Sat 22
Mon 17	Wed 19	Fri 21	

Ask and answer, like this:

> Are you free on Monday the 17th?
> No. I'm afraid I'm not.
> Well, are you free on Friday the 21st?
> Yes, I am.
> Oh good! I've got two tickets for ... Would you like to
>   come with me?
> Yes, I'd love to.

(Abbs and Freebairn 1982:70)

In the activity above, learners work with a framework of language which is very largely fixed in advance, so that through practice and repetition the learner can memorize expressions such as 'Would you like to...?', 'Yes, I'd love to', and so on. It makes sense to provide learners with some such phrases, because they perform useful social functions. (For discussion of such lexical phrases in learning and teaching, see Nattinger and DeCarrico (1992).) But, clearly, we cannot rely solely on this kind of activity. Learning grammar means learning to deploy language flexibly, combining elements from grammar and lexis in productive ways.

To help learners achieve this greater flexibility, we need activities which involve the active manipulation of language. Whereas noticing activities do not require tangible evidence that learners can do things with language, with structuring activities this is precisely what we do require. Of course, learners spend a great deal of classroom time doing things with language. However, we need to be careful here. To complete the activity on page 62, the learner certainly has to be active, but on closer inspection it is evident that all of this activity could be achieved with little, if any, understanding of the target grammar. Grammar is a prominent feature of the text, but it will not necessarily be prominent in the learner's response to the text.

It would be possible to correctly sequence the verb phrases solely by attending to the lexis, and making sense of the lexis by reference to the context established through the pictures. In short, the learner could process the entire activity top-down, disregarding the target grammar. None the less, some learners may become more aware of the two tenses featured in the story. Although completion of the exercise does not require great attention to grammar, equally it cannot prohibit it.

But it is worth being clear about the place of grammar in activities such as this. The learners are called on to work 'around' rather than 'with' the target grammar. There is an important distinction to be made here: between activities which have learners working around target grammar which has been carefully structured *for* the learner (as with the example above), and activities which require active structuring *by* the learner. Structuring by the learner means that she has to think for herself before she can correctly act on the grammatical rules and principles which product teaching focuses on. It means that the learner is not merely active, but actively involved. Some activities may be very brief and formal, yet they cannot be successfully negotiated without real thought. Others may be colourful, elaborate, and imaginative, yet on closer inspection they do not require a great deal of active involvement by the learner. Sometimes there is only a fine line between the two, with the learner having to think for herself, but only minimally.

Past Simple and Past Continuous

Narrating past events

PRESENTATION

Unfortunately this is a *true* story.
In January 1978 the firemen were on
strike, and the army took over the
job of answering emergency calls.

1 Here is a list of verbs in the *Past
Simple* which tell the events of the
story.
Look at the pictures and put the
verbs in the right order.
Number them 1–10.

- [ ] rescued
- [ ] arrived
- [ ] climbed
- [ ] killed
- [ ] called
- [ ] invited
- [ ] couldn't get down
- [ ] ran over
- [ ] put up (the ladder)
- [ ] offered

2 Here is a list of verbs in the *Past
Continuous* which describe the
scene of the narrative.
Look at the pictures and put the
verbs in the right order.
Letter them a–d.

- [ ] was waiting
- [ ] were leaving
- [ ] was working
- [ ] was playing

3 Now complete the story about
Mrs Brewin by putting a number
or a letter into each gap.

On 14 January 1978 Mrs Brewin
_____ in her garden. Her cat,
Henry, _____ around her. It _____
a tree in the garden and _____, so
she _____ the Fire Brigade. While
she _____ for them to arrive, she
_____ him some fish to try to get
him down.

The army finally _____, _____
their ladder and _____ the cat.
Mrs Brewin was delighted and
_____ them in for some tea. But as
they _____ ten minutes later, they
_____ the cat and _____ it.

● Grammar Question

What is the difference between the
Past Simple and the *Past Continuous*?

(Soars and Soars 1986:14)

▶ TASK 33

Each of the following activities involves manipulation of the grammar in some way. But which activities call for structuring *by* the learner, and which involve structuring *for* the learner? Are there any 'borderline' cases?

Activity 1

Question words and phrases

Complete the questions. Put in these words and phrases: **who, what, whose, where, when, what time, what colour, what kind, how often, how far, how long, how many.**

  □ *Where*   is Melbourne? ~ In Australia
  □ *What colour*   is the Greek flag? ~ Blue and white.
  1 _____ was the first President of the USA? ~ George
             Washington.
  2 _____ did the Second World War end? ~ In 1945.
  3 _____ inches are there in a foot? ~ Twelve.
  4 _____ do banks open in England? ~ Half past nine.
  5 _____ is a foal? ~ A young horse.
  6 _____ is it from San Francisco to Los Angeles? ~ About
             400 miles.
  7 _____ home is 10 Downing Street? ~ The Prime
             Minister's.
  8 _____ are the Olympic Games held? ~ Every four years.
  9 _____ of food is Cheddar? ~ Cheese.
  10 _____ is a game of rugby? ~ 80 minutes.

(*Eastwood 1992:59*)

Activity 2

---

7 Drill:
T: *Look at my watch. It was second-hand.*
T: *Was it? It doesn't look second-hand.*
T: *Look at my shoes. They were second-hand.*
T: *Were they? They don't look second-hand.*
T: *Look at my watch. It was second-hand.*
C: *Was it? It doesn't look second-hand.*

Continue:
Look at my shoes. They were second-hand.
Look at my bag. It was second-hand.
Look at my trousers. They were second-hand.
Look at my ring. It was second-hand.
Look at my pen. It was second-hand.

(*Hartley and Viney 1979: Unit 11*)

Activity 3

Passive sentences in various tenses; oral brainstorm; optionally, the structure *need*(s) *doing/to be done*.

Materials: Pairs of pictures showing a situation or place before and after a set of changes – like those in *Box 55*, for example.

Procedure: Ask the students to imagine that the second picture is the present and to describe what *has been done*. Or let them assume that the first is the present, and describe what they know *will be done* (i.e. the second picture). Or they can imagine that they are midway between the two, and describe what is in the process of *being done* in order for the situation in the first picture to change into the second. This can be done orally or in writing.

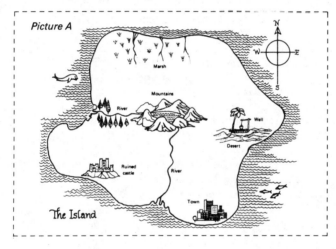

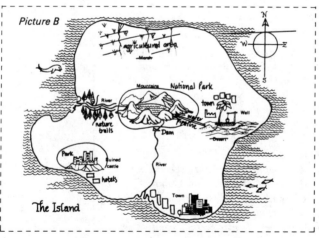

(Ur 1988:198–9)

Activity 4

---

1 Organise your class in threes and tell them they are going to compete in finding appropriate 'heads' for 14 'headless' sentences. Give out the sentence bodies. Set them a 7 minute time limit. Tell them to write in the sentence beginnings they think are correct.
2 When time is up pick one person from each triad and give them the sentence heads. Ask them to go back to a triad that is not their own and score that group's sentences.
3 Ask the scorers to tell their scores to the class and adjudicate on any points of doubt.

Sentence bodies (You need 1 per three students.)

.... is played by two or four people, often on grass.

.... is played with big men in parks in Germany.

.... is watched by millions more than play it.

.... a try can be converted into a goal.

.... is dominated by the Chinese.

.... is an event often won in the Olympics by black competitors.

.... is enjoyed in countries that used to be directly oppressed by Britain.

.... is/are played mainly by men in pubs.

.... tends to be played by rich people with a small, pitted ball.

.... are betted on by all sorts of people.

.... is played with nothing but a simple board and small round counters.

.... a man may not be hit below the belt.

.... is banned in China, but the Chinese love to play it.

.... the big balls have to end up as close as possible to the little ball.

(*Rinvolucri 1984:9–10*)

We cannot be too prescriptive in declaring one activity to be structured 'for the learner' and another activity to invite structuring 'by the learner'. The ultimate arbiter on these matters has to be the learner herself, and we can never legislate about how the learner will actually respond, or about what effects any particular activity may be having on the mental processing of individual learners. We can only make educated guesses. What matters is that we recognize the distinction, in principle, between these two broadly different types of activity, acknowledging that both have a role to play. Some learners may achieve a great deal with activities which require little engagement, and which may consequently help the learner to feel secure and untested. However, given that learning is of its nature an active process, learners should also demonstrate that they can think and act effectively through their own decision-making.

7.3 Grammar, context, and choice

In actual communication, language users choose what to say, and how to say it, depending on the context, as was outlined earlier in 3. Yet with none of the activities we examined in 7.2 does the learner have any genuine choice. Such activities present a static view of grammar: an object of study in isolation from the movement and change which is typical of grammar in language use. This isolation may well be beneficial, helping learners to carefully scrutinize and reflect on language form. But if we were to concentrate exclusively on this kind of approach, then we would be misrepresenting the nature of grammar in use. In actual contexts grammar is not a static object; it is a resource providing us with options from which we choose in order to signal our meanings effectively and appropriately. When learners practise a fixed dialogue in pairs, we are presenting them with the product of someone else's choices, a *fait accompli*. This is like showing them a package of target grammar to which is attached the label 'Communicative: look, but do not open'. A thoroughgoing exploitation of choice would take us into process teaching. None the less, it is possible to build an element of choice into a product framework, and we will now survey a number of ways in which this can be achieved.

▶ ## TASK 34

The following is a reworking of Activity 3 in Task 33 (Ur 1988). How does it allow for a degree of controlled choice by the learner? What kind of listening does it aim to develop?

Procedure: Students work in pairs. Student A looks at Picture B and decides which changes (1) have been made; (2) are in the process of being made; (3) will be made in the future.

Student A then communicates this information to student B, by saying (for example) 'A hotel is being built' or 'A national park has been opened'.

Student B listens and marks the information on her map: '1' for changes which have been made, '2' for changes being made, '3' for future changes.

By giving learners some responsibility for the choices they make, we aim to increase their active engagement with grammar as a functional device for signalling meaning. In Task 34, for instance, clarifying distinctions between past, present, and future hinges on attending to the choice of one form over another.

▶ TASK 35

The following information-gap activity has students working in pairs to practise prepositions of location. How might you adapt this task to introduce an element of guided choice, so that the learner chooses language to signal important distinctions in meaning?

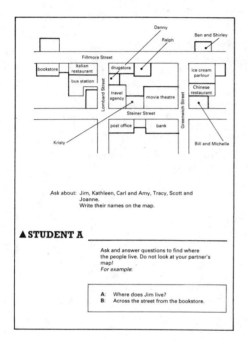

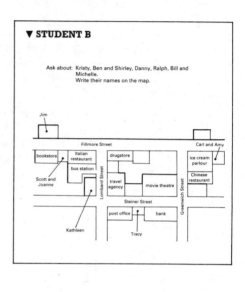

(*Harmer 1987:44*)

The choices which the learner makes with the reworked activity in Task 34 are to a large extent arbitrary: there is no particular reason why student A should select a past form in preference to a future form, beyond the fact that the activity requires her to do this. In language use, though, choices are not made in a contextual void; they are functionally motivated. We will put things a certain way for the good reason that it serves our particular and communicative purpose. So we should go further, and demonstrate to learners that choices are motivated in reference to specific situations of use.

▶ TASK 36

Each of the following three activities deals in some way with grammar as a resource for motivated choices. How is this achieved, and how far is the learner an active decision-maker in each case? What particular function of the grammar does each activity focus on?

Activity 1

In a set of statements, some of the words in one sentence are often repeated in other sentences. In passages, we try not to repeat words very often. We can refer back to words used in other sentences. This relation is called reference.

Study this short passage and notice the use of reference. This use of reference is shown in the diagram.

Deserts are very dry regions. They have very little rainfall. Few plants live there. Some specialized animals do. Some deserts have a surface of sand. The sand often forms dunes. These are created by the wind. Others have stones or rocks.

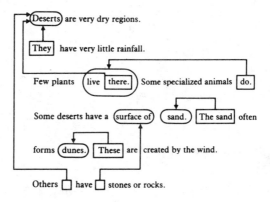

Draw a similar diagram to show the use of reference in the following passage.

Equatorial climates are found in some regions of the Equator. They have high temperatures and heavy rainfalls. Many plants live there. Daytime temperatures are about 26°C all the year. At night they may be 6°C below this. In most of these areas rainfall is about 50 inches a year. In some it is more than 200 inches.

(*Reading and Thinking in English* 1979:14–15)

Activity 2

> Rewrite the passage below so that it is easier to read. Try to use short words such as *we*, *this*, *there*, and *he*. Assume that your reader already knows the following:
>
> – that you are writing about a recent holiday you took with a group of friends;
> – that you stayed at a hotel called 'The Sunset Paradise'.
>
> 'My friends and I arrived at a hotel called 'The Sunset Paradise' at around 7.00. My friends and I went over to the reception desk and told the man behind the reception desk that my friends and I had made a reservation. The man behind the reception desk declared that he had no record of the reservation we had just mentioned to him. I said that the fact that there was no record of the reservation was ridiculous.'

Activity 3

> Work your way through the following passage, deciding for each new sentence whether version 'a' or 'b' is the most suitable continuation.
>
> Weathering and erosion of rock exposed to the atmosphere constantly remove particles from the rock.
>
> | a | b | c |
> |---|---|---|
> | 1 These rock particles are called sediment. | Sediment is what these rock particles are called. | What these rock particles are called is sediment. |
>
> | a | b |
> |---|---|
> | 2 The upper layers press down on the lower ones as sediments accumulate. | As sediments accumulate, the upper layers press down on the lower ones. |
>
> | a | b |
> |---|---|
> | 3 Sediments that stick together form sedimentary rocks. | Sedimentary rocks are formed by sediments that stick together. |
>
> | a | b |
> |---|---|
> | 4 Such rocks have been able to survive the test of time only in this way. | Only in this way have such rocks been able to survive the test of time. |

(*Rutherford 1987:163*; my rubric added)

By revealing grammar as a device for communicative decision-making, we are seeking to promote the learner's self-discovery of grammar as a resource for choice. This brings us once again to consciousness-raising, because consciousness-raising is:

'...the means to an end, not the end itself. That is, whatever it is that is raised to consciousness is not to be looked upon as an artifact or object of study ... Rather, what is raised to consciousness is not the grammatical product but aspects of the grammatical process...'
(*Rutherford 1987:104*)

In Task 36 we were concerned with transactional grammar: with how a writer can choose to grammaticize a text in reference to shared knowledge, and across sentence boundaries. But, as we saw in **4.6**, grammar is also a resource for choice in the social context, a device for constructing and expressing our attitudes and our relationships with each other.

▶ TASK 37

1 How does the following activity focus on grammar in a social context? Which particular forms and social function are being highlighted?

Here is a part of a dialogue between two people who share a flat.

A: These windows are disgusting! They look like they haven't been cleaned for months.
B: You mean *you* haven't cleaned them.
A: Well, I'm not sure that it was decided who would clean them, was it?
B: Yes it was, my love. We agreed that you would look after the windows down here. Remember?
A: Well, you could be right I suppose. OK, I'll make sure it gets done.

(a) What kind of relationship do you think they have with each other? Where are they?

(b) Working with a partner, tick (i) or (ii) in the following table:

When A says ...	A means ...
These windows ... look like they haven't been cleaned for months.	(i) I'd like *you* to clean them. (ii) They need cleaning.
I'm not sure that it was decided who would clean them, was it?	(i) I want to avoid agreeing to clean them. (ii) We haven't discussed this yet.
I'll make sure it gets done.	(i) I promise to clean them myself. (ii) I might ask someone else to clean them.

(c) Do you notice any grammatical forms which are used to express the meanings you chose in (b)?

(d) With your partner, plan a similar dialogue on a different subject and using different characters.

2 How might a similar approach be taken to demonstrate other context-sensitive grammatical functions which were discussed in 3?

This perspective on grammar, where the forms are presented in direct association with the contexts in which they are chosen, remains relatively uncommon in language teaching materials. This is unfortunate, because it helps us to represent grammar as it is used—as a communicative resource for choice.

7.4 Product teaching in perspective

No single approach to language teaching can hope to be completely effective, and product teaching is no exception. Like other approaches, it has its drawbacks as well as its strengths. In terms of strengths, it provides a clear framework—an outline of the language points to be covered. Such a structured approach can give learners a strong sense of direction, and this in itself can have a motivating effect. It allows learners to focus their attention on specific aspects of the language system, without all the additional demands of real-time language use. Research suggests that product teaching can promote quite rapid learning of explicit grammatical forms, and in so doing can contribute to a high level of ultimate achievement. See the discussion in Larsen-Freeman and Long (1991:312–21).

Another positive feature of product teaching is its flexibility. Once particular grammatical forms have been targeted by the syllabus designer, the teacher still has very considerable scope in deciding how these items should be revealed to the learners. We can, for example, vary the emphasis given to form and meaning, concentrating at times on formal aspects of the language system (as with a number of the activities in Task 33), at other times focusing on specific functions of the grammar. Teachers can also vary the emphasis from time to time between explicit direction provided for the learners, and a more careful encouragement of active involvement and self-discovery by the learners. All teaching must, by definition, involve a measure of guidance: to provide no guidance at all would be to abdicate any responsibility for teaching. What matters is how much guidance to provide, and in what way. With both noticing and structuring activities, we can choose how much to give to the learner, and how much to require of the learner. With structuring activities the element of active involvement and learner decision-making can be extended to the point where principled grammatical choices are being made, albeit in a carefully controlled way. These issues can be summarized as follows:

Noticing for the learner	Noticing by the learner
Learners are presented with explicitly formulated information about forms and their functions (e.g. Task 29, Extract 1)	Learners are guided to work out for themselves information about forms and their functions (e.g. Task 30, Activity 1)

Structuring for the learner		Structuring by the learner
Mechanical manipulation or repetition of forms. (e.g. Task 32)	Learners have to think for themselves so as to manipulate forms correctly (e.g. Task 33, Activity 1)	Learners have to process or manipulate forms as choice to make meanings clear (e.g. Task 36, Activity 3)

Figure 8

This flexibility is sometimes overlooked by critics of product teaching, who discuss it is as if it were largely a matter of learners mechanically manipulating forms. One critical account, for example, talks of the problems involved in asking learners to 'repeat and over-learn forms which have no associated meaning' (Lightbown 1983b:239). We should be careful not to over-generalize from such criticisms, which may well apply only to the most highly controlled and constrained kind of product teaching.

And yet there are limitations to product teaching, however imaginatively it is conceived. No matter how ingeniously we contrive tasks for noticing and structuring grammar, we can never be sure that all this activity will lead to the real pay-off: the ability to process and use grammar in real-life communication, with learners navigating their own way through the unpredictabilities of the discourse traffic. With product teaching these unpredictabilities—the changes in the roles participants play, in the topics they deal with, in their patterns of interaction, and in the time pressure they are under—are taken out, and for good reason. Even with the more context-sensitive activities we have just considered, it is only selected features of language use which the learners work with: we have not yet allowed them to put it all together for themselves.

A product approach offers no explicit opportunity for proceduralization (discussed in 5.4), whereby knowledge becomes internalized to the point where it can be drawn on more or less automatically. There is no clear evidence from research that product teaching can achieve this. On the contrary, a number of studies seem to indicate that with respect to many key grammatical forms, product teaching has little effect on spontaneous language use. See, for example, Ellis (1984), Kadia (1988), and for a general review Ellis (1990:161–6). Proceduralization requires sustained practice in using grammar when the reins have been loosened, and when learners are negotiating their own meanings. For this we must turn to consider process teaching.

8   Teaching grammar as process

8.1 Process activity or process teaching?

Process teaching engages learners directly in the procedures of language use. But we do not simply throw them in at the deep end, letting them do whatever they like with no control or guidance whatsoever. We use, though, a very different kind of guidance from product teaching. Instead of targeting specific features of the grammar for the learner's attention, now we are explicitly aiming to develop the skills and strategies of the discourse process, constructing tasks which learners can use to express themselves more effectively as discourse participants. In process teaching we do not only want them to achieve the self-discovery which is facilitated by consciousness-raising, but also the self-expression of language use.

The kind of process teaching discussed here is sometimes referred to as 'task-based'. Candlin (1987) offers a detailed taxonomy for the qualities of 'good' tasks, including the following:

- they encourage learners to attend to meaning and to purposeful language use
- they give learners flexibility in resolving problems their own way, calling on their own choice of strategies and skills
- they *involve* learners, with their own personalities and attitudes being central
- they are challenging, yet not excessively demanding
- they raise learners' awareness of the processes of language use, and encourage them to reflect on their own language use.

▶   TASK 38

What do you think are the specific justifications for each of Candlin's requirements listed above? Bearing these in mind, which of the following two activities most clearly involves a process, i.e. task-based, approach?

Activity 1

Have a look at the photograph below. It accompanied an article in *The Guardian* of Monday, June 23, 1980.

Life on earth continued yesterday despite torrential rain which did nothing to dampen the determination of protesters at London's nuclear disarmament rally.

Discuss the following questions very briefly in your group. Then report to the class.

- What was the purpose of the demonstration?
- What do you think of the way in which these people are trying to achieve their goal?
- Will they be successful? Why (not)?
- If you had not seen the photograph, would you have understood the text under it?
- Which elements in this photograph would inspire you, if you wanted to make a poster protesting against nuclear armament?
- What would you have thought if this letter had appeared in *The Guardian* of June 25?

(*Grellet, Maley, and Welsing 1983:66*)

Activity 2

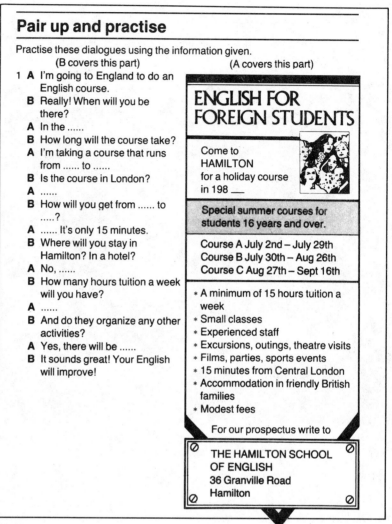

Pair up and practise

Practise these dialogues using the information given.

(B covers this part)   (A covers this part)

1 **A** I'm going to England to do an
    English course.
  B Really! When will you be
    there?
  A In the ......
  B How long will the course take?
  A I'm taking a course that runs
    from ...... to ......
  B Is the course in London?
  A ......
  B How will you get from ...... to
    .....?
  A ...... It's only 15 minutes.
  B Where will you stay in
    Hamilton? In a hotel?
  A No, ...
  B How many hours tuition a week
    will you have?
  A ......
  B And do they organize any other
    activities?
  A Yes, there will be ......
  B It sounds great! Your English
    will improve!

ENGLISH FOR FOREIGN STUDENTS

Come to
HAMILTON
for a holiday course
in 198 __

Special summer courses for
students 16 years and over.

Course A July 2nd – July 29th
Course B July 30th – Aug 26th
Course C Aug 27th – Sept 16th

* A minimum of 15 hours tuition a
  week
* Small classes
* Experienced staff
* Excursions, outings, theatre visits
* Films, parties, sports events
* 15 minutes from Central London
* Accommodation in friendly British
  families
* Modest fees

For our prospectus write to

THE HAMILTON SCHOOL
OF ENGLISH
36 Granville Road
Hamilton

(Richards and Long 1985:25)

You may wish to refer back to Candlin's factors later when assessing some of the other tasks we will look at in the light of his criteria.

Imagine, then, a fictional teacher who has recently devoted considerable time to the teaching of the past tense through product work: it has been presented and practised in all manner of ways, used in all sorts of ways in dialogues and drills, in groups and in pairs. Subsequently, the teacher decides to loosen the reins, giving learners the chance to express themselves more freely in process work. With this objective she gives them the following task:

> Look at these pictures. They are about Freddy and something
> which happened to him last week on his desert island. Tell
> this story to your partner using your own words. See who can
> tell the story in the shortest time.

(Pictures from *Ur 1988:216*)

Figure 9

The teacher withdraws to the back of the class with fingers crossed. She
hopes that the learners will now produce the past tense in their own
language. But she hopes in vain. The following is typical of the language
they produce:

'Freddy is he has sit tree ... look his glasses and ... is happy jump ... girl
then she come and ... er ... sign this man ... then after that he have very
much water and ... is very sad I think.'

The learners' speech is rambling and faltering. Features of the narrative
come and go with no clear focus, and there is no evidence of the past
tense (so carefully rehearsed in product work), nor indeed of very much
grammatical elaboration at all.

This is not an example of process teaching, but merely of process activity. The teacher had given no thought to the effects of the task on the learners' performance. She had thought only that it was time to release control and to 'see what happens'. Process *activity*, then, refers to the unregulated production of language by learners who are unaware or unsure of the purpose underlying their performance. It may, as with the Freddie story, result from an activity which is poorly or inconsiderately constructed. Alternatively, it may involve an absence of any attempt to regulate what learners are doing and why they are doing it, as would be the case with free conversation. Process *teaching*, in contrast, requires careful attention to task design, so that we can make principled decisions about the effects of the task on learner language. In particular, we will want learners to take every opportunity to deploy grammar in their talk, stretching their linguistic resources so that they use language which is grammatically rich. This procedure is sometimes referred to as 'interlanguage stretching', and it requires learners to 'operate at the outer limits of their current abilities' (Long 1989:13).

Interlanguage stretching requires a careful regulation of task design. Without such regulation, we will be involved not in principled process teaching, but in unprincipled process activity. The danger of the latter is that learners will consistently fail to stretch their language, ultimately proceduralizing a very limited language system, as was noted in **5.6**.

8.2 Regulating language use

We begin with a fundamental premise: that language use is not one skill but many, as we saw in **5.4**. Competent language users manage to cope with this because some of these skills have become automatic. In particular, they have learned to proceduralize their language knowledge so they can use it without giving it undue attention, paying more heed instead to meaning. Learners, though, will not be able to achieve this level of skill without considerable practice and guidance. Human beings are limited in their capacity to consciously attend to more than one task at a time (Shiffrin and Schneider 1977). So it will be difficult for learners to attend simultaneously both to the quality of their language and to the meanings they are expressing. Something has to give way, and very often it is grammar which is the first thing to be surrendered. So, what kinds of factors can help us to regulate learner language to prevent features of the grammar being abandoned in this way?

With the activity in Figure 9 there were two key factors which were inadequately regulated. The first is pressure: the teacher had effectively set out to put the pressure on, by imposing an imperative to complete the task as quickly as possible. But the more pressure learners are under, the less time will be available for them to collect their thoughts. Time pressure is an important element in task design, and in **8.3** and **8.4** we will look more closely at how it can be regulated to influence the quality of learner language.

The second key factor has more to do with meaning: the teacher had wanted her learners to use the past simple tense, yet it was made clear to everyone from the outset that the narrative took place in the past. It was, then, part of the learners' initial shared knowledge, spelt out in the rubric to the task: the pictures 'are about Freddy and something which happened to him last week'. So why should learners trouble to waste scarce resources to signal something which would be communicatively redundant? As we have already seen, the more shared knowledge there is, the less need there is for meanings to be made clear through the use of grammar. Here, then, is another important factor for task design: the regulation of shared knowledge. This is discussed in 8.5 and 8.6.

Regulation in process teaching is a much more subtle kind of control than that which is exercised in product teaching. Instead of simply blocking out major aspects of language use, we are influencing and shaping certain features of context more indirectly, in the hope that this will lead to a corresponding effect on the grammar which learners use. Interestingly enough, airline pilots are given a similar kind of regulation. Long before they climb into the cockpit and take several hundred lives into their hands, they spend hundreds of hours in a simulator, where specific features of the context are deliberately varied: speed, weather conditions, the amount of competing air traffic. All these are factors which computers regulate so that trainee pilots can learn to cope with them simultaneously in real-time flying conditions. In aviation this skill is known as 'time-sharing'.

Carefully regulated process work can give learners repeated opportunities to notice and restructure their working hypotheses about language, as well as to progressively proceduralize this knowledge. But the very fact that they are deploying their own language, with its inevitable inconsistencies, means that there must be limits to the accuracy of their restructuring process, and therefore to the accuracy of the language which they proceduralize. We should not, then, hold unreasonable expectations of process teaching. Our objective is not to carefully control the learner's accurate production of grammatical forms—this is the domain of product teaching. Rather, it is to develop the skill of exploiting grammar to express meanings as clearly as possible in language use. This in itself is a major objective, and it takes time to accomplish. The culture of the process classroom is a very different one from the product classroom, with learners having much greater responsibility for their own language production. We cannot legislate in advance about which particular forms will be used in a task, or about the precision with which they are deployed. If we think of process teaching as a risky and time-consuming way of getting learners to formulate specific forms which can be focused on much more economically in product work, then we are misrepresenting the very nature of process teaching. Learning is learner-centred, and it follows that whatever we do in the classroom is conditioned by the learner's individual motivation and need to use grammar.

In many ways the objectives of product and process teaching are complementary. The focus in process teaching is on the learner's own self-expression, and consequently we cannot directly intervene to focus on this or that grammatical form. In product teaching exactly the reverse situation applies. Effective grammar teaching is likely to involve a combination of both approaches, as was argued in **6**.

We now need to consider how to implement process teaching. We will concentrate for the most part on speaking tasks, where communicative pressure is likely to be at its greatest, and where effective re-structuring and proceduralization will therefore be difficult to achieve.

8.3   Regulating time pressure

We have all experienced the dislocation that pressure can bring to bear on our language production. Attending an interview for a job we want very much, we may find ourselves struggling unimpressively to get our language out—slips of the tongue and endless 'ums' and 'ers' clutter our performance. When it's all over, we re-run crucial moments in our mind's eye with the thought 'If only I'd said this instead of that'. How much more strenuous the whole experience of spontaneous language use must be for the learner, and particularly for those learners whose personality does not incline them towards self-expression under the critical gaze of a teacher and fellow students.

One solution is disarmingly simple: give learners, quite explicitly, time to plan what they are going to produce. In one study on this subject, it was found that giving learners planning time led them to produce language with a much wider range of vocabulary and more varied grammatical patterns than was the case when no planning time was permitted (Crookes 1989). In another study, reported by Ellis (1987), learners were given three kinds of task: a planned writing task, a planned speaking task, and an unplanned speaking task. The study found that learners used grammar to signal regular past with greatest accuracy in the planned writing task, less accurately in the planned speaking task, and least of all in the unplanned speaking task. Of course, the process of writing generally provides much more opportunity to pause for thought than does speaking, so it is not surprising that the planned writing task led to the most accurate production. Here, again, there is evidence that planning time reduces pressure and so allows learners time to collect their thoughts and to bring grammar under more effective control.

▶ TASK 39

Here are two extracts from Ellis's data. One is from the planned writing task, the other from the planned speaking task. Which is which? What differences do you note between the two in terms of the grammar used? Consider, in particular, relative clauses, and the past and past perfect tenses.

Extract 1
The policeman was in this corner whistle but it was too late. The two thieves escape with the big suitcase, took their car and went in the traffic. They passed near a zoo and stop in a forest. There they had a big surprise. The basket contain a snake.

Extract 2
A policeman who was there whistled. But it was too late. The thief and his young collaborator had taken a car and had disappeared on the traffic. They stopped on a forest but they had haven a big surprise when they opened the case. It contained a big snake and they knew nothing.

(Adapted from *Ellis 1987:10*)

As is evident from Ellis's data, planning time makes it easier for the learner to activate her existing knowledge, giving her more opportunity to stretch her language resources, and hence to restructure, and ultimately to proceduralize, a more accurate working system. So there is a very strong argument for building opportunities for planning into classroom tasks.

▶ TASK 40

1 What devices are used in these two activities to give learners time to plan? Might one approach work better with your learners than the other?

Activity 1

In groups, look at the picture below and discuss what you think is happening, and how people feel.

Now work alone and imagine you are one of the people in the picture. Write an account in your diary of what happened that day. Use some of the following adverbs:
at first   then   later on   afterwards   soon   finally   at last.

Here are some guidelines:
guests/arrive
have drinks/have lunch
relax/spend a quiet afternoon talking
be hot
have a swim/a pool
an accident/whirlpool sucking in swimmers
shouts/screams/panic
be frightened/hurt/startled/embarrassed

"This always has to happen when we've got company."

(*Boutin, Brinand, and Grellet 1987:10–11*)

Activity 2

CREATIVE WRITING

This photograph shows an example of the damage caused by the storm which you heard about at the beginning of the unit.

1   You are going to write the telephone conversation the man is having in the telephone box. Use your imagination and decide:

a) who the man is speaking to.
b) what has happened. Give details.
c) what he has decided to do.

2   Quickly make a draft version of the telephone dialogue. Remember to use contracted forms (e.g. *'I've got a problem.'* NOT *'I have got a problem.'*). (You may want to use some of the 'telephone vocabulary' practised in the section above.)

3   Show your draft to another student. How can it be improved? Are the spelling and punctuation correct? Ask for suggestions.

4   Rewrite the dialogue as carefully as you can.

5   Act out the dialogues.

(*Bell and Gower* 1991:38)

2 Skehan (1994) suggests that learners might use planning time in different ways: some to prepare their ideas (planning meaning), others to think more about their language content (planning form). Do you think that either of the above activities would influence the type of planning which the learner does?

We should think of planning time not merely as a one-off technique which we use occasionally, but as an approach to the design of tasks over entire courses. Prabhu (1987) has an approach in which almost every classroom task is preceded by what he calls a 'pre-task', where learners rehearse some of the cognitive demands of the task itself. But we do not want our learners to become over-dependent on planning time: our aim is to ease them gradually into the pressures on real-time language use. We could, then, consider ways of progressively reducing preparation time, so that the pressure of spontaneous use gradually appears less daunting.

▶   TASK 41

Here are some ways of manipulating planning time over a series of lessons. How effective and practical would each one be for your learners? To what extent can these ideas be combined? What ideas could you add to the list?

1 Providing time for written preparation, with learners using written notes as they perform; then asking them to put their notes away in the actual task; then allowing only oral preparation; then, finally, no preparation.

2 Beginning with preparation in groups, then later asking individuals to prepare on their own.

3 Gradually reducing the time available for preparation, whatever form it takes.

4 Gradually reducing the time available for the performance of the task itself.

5 For listening activities, letting learners refer to a written transcript as they listen (and/or 'pausing' the tape as they listen) and progressively reducing the time they have to refer to the transcript (or reducing the frequency and length of pauses).

One question which remains largely unanswered is the effect of planning time on more dynamic, interactive activities. Here we have to be careful; too much planning might only serve to constrain the very dynamism and unpredictability which learners will need experience in handling. Yet there are still possibilities. Di Pietro (1987) offers what he calls a 'strategic interaction' approach to classroom interaction. Here learners get plenty of time to plan and even rehearse a scene or role-play, but when they actually perform the piece, new and unexpected information is added, calling for an alert response and a quick change of direction.

► TASK 42

In the following activity learners are given a very clear framework on which to base a dialogue. How might you adapt it so that, having planned or rehearsed the role-play, learners are called on to negotiate some unexpected developments?

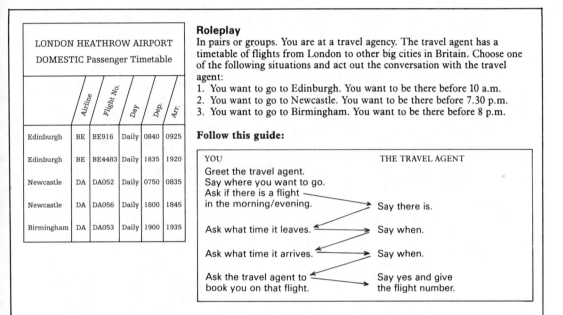

Roleplay

In pairs or groups. You are at a travel agency. The travel agent has a timetable of flights from London to other big cities in Britain. Choose one of the following situations and act out the conversation with the travel agent:

1. You want to go to Edinburgh. You want to be there before 10 a.m.
2. You want to go to Newcastle. You want to be there before 7.30 p.m.
3. You want to go to Birmingham. You want to be there before 8 p.m.

Follow this guide:

YOU	THE TRAVEL AGENT
Greet the travel agent.	
Say where you want to go.	
Ask if there is a flight in the morning/evening.	Say there is.
Ask what time it leaves.	Say when.
Ask what time it arrives.	Say when.
Ask the travel agent to book you on that flight.	Say yes and give the flight number.

(*Abbs and Freebairn 1982:50*)

By building in an element of unexpected deviation, we can encourage learners to activate grammar under pressure, when they have to improvise and assemble their language at speed. But if they are used to working with controlled dialogues such as the one above, then even a seemingly minor alteration may appear to materialize out of the blue, and be received as a very alarming and unwelcome development. What we should aim for is an approach where the actual changes are unexpected, but where the practice of dealing with change is a predictable and regular feature of the course.

So time pressure can be regulated by varying planning time and through controlling the time available to perform the task itself. How much time to provide can only be judged by the teacher, with reference to a particular group of learners. It would certainly be naïve to say 'The more time, the better the language'. Learners will have their own optimum level of time pressure—the point where they can stretch their language without feeling either over-pressurized (too little time) or not pressurized enough (too much time). It should be possible for teachers to progressively step up the pressure over a series of lessons, as the class becomes more accustomed to the competing demands of time and effective language production.

8.4 Regulating topic and familiarity

Providing space for planning creates a sense of familiarity with what will follow, and familiarity can strongly influence the quality of the language produced and attended to. Another way in which familiarity can be exploited is through giving learners topics for discussion which they are already familiar with so that, as with planning time, they have more mental space to attend to the quality of their own and each other's language. See Anderson and Lynch: *Listening*, pages 49–50 for discussion of topic familiarity in the listening process.

This can be done in a number of ways. One strategy is to ask learners to talk about a topic with which they are already familiar from their life experiences. English for Specific Purposes teachers, for instance, often report that their learners are highly motivated to explain quite technical aspects of their work with which others in the class are not familiar. Another strategy is to provide opportunities for revisiting a topic or theme which has aready occurred earlier in the course. In both cases we are giving learners the chance to re-encounter and to develop particular language routines without the added pressure created by working with novel or unfamiliar material. It is exactly under conditions like these that restructuring and proceduralization can be driven forward. It may be that we are too concerned with variety and novelty in the topics we select for classroom work, and that we should consider more carefully the case for including material which is familiar and comfortable to learners.

But of course, there is always the danger that the learner will simply sit back in these circumstances, comfortable in the knowledge that the topic presents her with no great problems, but not particularly motivated to use the available time to make her language richer. So we need to think about how we can regulate familiarity, keeping learners alert to the language they are working with. One possibility here is to integrate a careful selection of topic with a regulation of planning time. The teacher might choose an unfamiliar theme but give learners plenty of time to prepare their ideas in advance. Alternatively, this procedure could be reversed, so that a familiar theme is provided but relatively little planning time is permitted.

▶ TASK 43

How are planning time and topic combined in the following activity?

Select one of the following:

- one of the topics from Unit 1.2 Task 1 page 2
- the history or geography of your region/town
- your hobby (e.g. photography)
- a process you know a lot about (e.g. wine-making).

If possible, choose something the others in your class are interested in but know little about.

Prepare a 3-minute talk on your topic. Make notes and, if possible, select pictures which will illustrate your points.

(*Gower 1987:11*)

It is interesting to consider the activity in Task 43 from the point of view of listening. The suggestion that learners should select a topic which others in the class 'are interested in but know little about' means that there could be a genuinely communicative motivation for the rest of the class to attend as each student speaks. In other words, what is familiar to the speaker will be less familiar to the listener, and thus their shared knowledge will be limited. This raises the question of the particular meanings which learners are signalling through their language use, which we will consider in 8.5.

The precise effects of this kind of regulation will depend on the learners' tolerance of pressure, their interest in particular topics, and their capacity to handle the unfamiliar without serious disruption of their language. As we saw in 8.3, learners are likely to have an optimum level of pressure, where a certain amount of available time, in alliance with a topic which is more or less familiar, will encourage a stretching of their language resources. Over a period of time, tolerance to pressure—and hence a capacity to handle language use in closer approximation to real-time conditions—should increase. Very roughly, then, the procedure is as follows:

Less pressure   **More pressure**

Familiar topic, considerable time to plan	Familiar topic, little or no time to plan	Unfamiliar topic, with no planning time
	OR	
	Unfamiliar topic, planning time available	

Figure 10

8.5 Regulating shared knowledge: context-gap

We have seen, then, that under the pressure of real-time language use, learners will very often find themselves unable to simultaneously manage all the skills required. Yet this does not mean that they will dispense with grammar entirely. Instead they may dispense with just those aspects of the grammar which are redundant because they would only signal meanings which were already self-evident. It makes sense, in short, for learners to concentrate resources on those points which need to be communicated because they are not part of shared knowledge.

The learner who is too reliant on a supporting context will have great difficulty in spelling out her meaning in situations where shared knowledge cannot be relied upon to come to her aid. She runs the risk of becoming so used to avoiding certain aspects of the grammar that they disappear from her working system altogether. She will get into the habit of evading grammar, so that what gets proceduralized is a language system which relies much more on lexis than on grammar, as with 'man walk street', 'plane fly sky', and so on. We need to consider how we can push learners beyond the stage of getting their message across, because otherwise they will not greatly develop their underlying knowledge of the language system (see the argument in Skehan (1994)). According to Swain: 'Simply getting one's message across can and does occur with grammatically deviant forms . . . Negotiating meaning needs to incorporate the notion of being pushed towards the delivery of a message that is not only conveyed, but that is conveyed precisely, coherently and appropriately' (1985:248–9).

In process teaching, of course, the precision of learner language has to be contingent on the context of the task in question, and on the motivation and limitations of the learners themselves. Nevertheless, we can push learners to use language with greater precision through exploiting the principle of shared knowledge. If learners reduce the quantity and quality of their language in response to information which is already shared between them, then this can be countered by building into tasks a need to make certain meanings clear which are not already self-evident. In essence, they will share knowledge through the performance of the task, rather than rely entirely on knowledge which is shared from the outset of the task.

In product teaching this is achieved through information-gap activities. Typically, these require the careful distribution of information between, say, two learners who then have to share their respective knowledge through the carefully controlled exchange of question and answer (as, for example, with the activity in Task 35). In process teaching this level of control is inappropriate. Instead, we want to motivate learners to make their own meanings clear. So, in place of the traditional notion of an information-gap, we might think instead of a *context-gap*. Context-gap is the gap in knowledge between what is known, and known to be known, between all learners at the outset of a process task, and the knowledge which they need to clearly express to complete the activity. Context-gaps can be created and regulated in various ways, without at the same time controlling the specific forms which learners will use.

► ## TASK 44

How much of a context-gap is there likely to be in the following activity, and how might this depend on the learner's background and culture?

Love story

They fly off to the Caribbean for their honeymoon.

She takes him home to meet her parents, and he does the same.

They get married, and invite all their friends and relations to the wedding.

John and Mary meet at a party. A friend introduces them.

They start going out together regularly.

They decide to get engaged, and he buys her a diamond ring.

They move into a small flat together.

1 **Work in pairs. Put the story in the most likely order.**

2 **Do you like the story as it is? Make up your own version. Change it in any way you like.**

They have a baby daughter, and they call her Anna, after Mary's mother.

He invites her out to see a film, and afterwards they have dinner together.

(*Doff and Jones 1991:13*)

Every task in process teaching presupposes a context-gap of some kind; every process task, that is, creates a partial or incomplete context—a problem to solve, an argument to conclude. The learner's job is to complete the task by reducing or eliminating the context-gap through language use. A proper regulation of context-gap calls for careful thought— the task designer needs to consider what exactly is unclear or unavailable when the task commences, and how the learners can be motivated to discover and share this information. This means getting a suitable balance between two extremes: on the one hand, avoiding an over-rigorous control of learner language (this would be product teaching), while avoiding texts and tasks which are so ambiguous that the learner is left wondering what she is required to do, and why (this would be process activity as defined in **8.1**).

▶ TASK 45

How does each of the following activities establish a context-gap? What kind of balance is struck between controlling the learner's choice and leaving them free (or too free) to construct their own responses? How important will the learner's personality and culture be?

Activity 1

---

61. Communication Problems

Sorry, what did you say?

Sorry?

I didn't get the bit about...

I'm sorry I can't hear you. It's a very bad line.

It is very easy to misunderstand someone on the telephone. We can't see the person we are speaking to. The line can be bad. There may be other noises around us. In this difficult situation, we use the phrases in the list.

Work in pairs with these serious situations. Correct communication is essential. One student is the telephone receptionist for emergencies. Take it in turns to be the caller.

One of the situations provided:

Think of an emergency situation which you have been involved in yourself. Act out the situation with a telephone receptionist.

(Keller and Warner 1988:82–3)

Activity 2

Make up a story

Can you make up a story to fit these pictures? You can put them in any order you like.

Write some notes to help you tell your story.

Read out your story and see if people can say what order the pictures are in.

(*Willis and Willis 1988:95*)

Activity 3

SPEAKING

Story telling

Work in groups. You are going to tell a story about a man who was found unconscious in a tube train. Choose at least one of the words from both A and B below and one of the items in each of C and D and decide on your story line. Practise telling the story, adding as many ideas as you like.

A

| blood stain first-aid kit |
| bandage   the 'kiss of life' |

B

| ambulance   jogging |
| police station   reward |

(*Bell and Gower 1991:67*)

8.6 Context-gap: reasoning and world-creating

Involved in an argument or a debate, we may find ourselves using quite complex language, because we are concerned to get over and justify our point of view, as with 'I believe that . . .', 'because . . .', 'but if we don't . . .', 'then . . .', 'If what you say is true, then . . .', and so on. Engaged in a debate, we reason, explain, and justify our ideas, and perhaps check and evaluate them in relation to the points raised by others. During this kind of reasoning, quite complex and elaborate grammar gets used as we are called on to search for evidence and justifications. Duff (1986) suggests that learners as well as proficient users tend to elaborate their grammar quite extensively when they are asked to debate and reason in this way.

▶ TASK 46

In her research, Duff recorded some intermediate-level learners who were asked to have a debate on the question of whether television is a good or a bad thing. In the following extract, can you see how this learner's use of grammar seems to bear out Duff's hypothesis?

'OK I think TV is good because it's a—you see—you can let people know—more things about the world. This is very useful very helpful people. So they can just sit at home and know everything—happened in their state in their country—even in the world—SPACE! What do you think?'

(*Duff 1986:177*)

It is reasoning which is the key here. When we ask our learners to explain and justify, we are drawing them into an inner world of their own making. They are not simply describing a picture or saying what they did last weekend. Instead, they are creating a world which is independent of the world around them, conjuring up ideas which have to do with possible futures and unreal conditions. Here we have a whole range of world-creating forms, including conditionals, clauses and conjuncts to signal cause, and so on. When learners reach into their own mental worlds, they are automatically working in a world where little knowledge can be assumed to be shared. In debates and arguments learners are naturally inclined to 'diverge'—keeping some opposition and distance between each other. As long as they persist in diverging, there will inevitably be a context-gap between them, with each learner having to make her own viewpoint clear and, perhaps, seeking to persuade others that her opinion is valid. As we saw in **4.4**, it would be very difficult to express such thoughts without the aid of grammar. So if we can encourage learners to use reasoned argument or debate in the tasks we design, then we will be encouraging them to exploit grammar as a necessary device for their self-expression.

But there are many kinds of reasoning, and the kind of reasoning we do will inevitably affect the language we use to signal it. If, for instance, we are busily trying to work out where on earth we last saw the car keys, we may catch ourselves using the language of deduction: 'They can't be in the sitting room because . . ., but I could have left them at work because . . .'. If we are discussing how to deal with pollution, we may well use clauses of purpose: 'We should do this so that/in order to . . .'. When we call on our learners to reason in some way, it is worth considering just what kind of reasoning will be required because that will have an effect on the kind of language they use.

► **TASK 47**

There are many kinds of classroom activities which can include a reasoning component. How do the following activities encourage learners to use the language of reasoning, and what kind of reasoning is involved in each case?

Activity 1

Puzzle

INTERNATIONAL TIME

Gill lives in London, but has a good friend in San Francisco. They occasionally ring each other up.
Gill's friend is out at work all day, usually from 8 a.m. to 5.45 p.m., and she also goes out quite a lot in the evenings. There is 8 hours' time difference between the two countries in the winter, London being ahead of San Francisco.

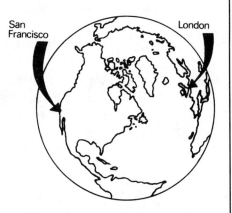

What time would be best for Gill to phone her friend?

Do other people in your class agree with your choice?

 Write down the time you decide on, and your reason for choosing it.

(*Willis and Willis 1988:88*)

Activity 2

Persuasion

Task 1

> *Either*
> Write down three things you hate doing (e.g. swimming underwater).
>
> In groups, exchange lists and select one item from the list you are given.
>
> Pair up with the person who wrote it. Imagine the situation and try and persuade him/her to do the thing they hate doing. You are his/her friend.
>
> *or*
> Write down three objects you can never imagine yourself buying (e.g. a space suit).
>
> In groups, exchange lists. Select one item from the list you are given.
>
> Pair up with the person who wrote it. Imagine the situation and try to persuade him/her to buy the object they do not want. You have a large stock!

(*Gower 1987:10–11*)

▶ **TASK 48**

The following pictures involve a plot rich in ambiguous motivations for people's actions. Think about how you might exploit them for a reasoning activity. What kind of reasoning might learners be drawn towards?

1

2

3

4

5

6

(*Gower 1987:45*)

But some learners may feel thoroughly uncomfortable with activities which ask them to dispute with fellow students, to the point where they fail to involve themselves at all in the activity, defeating the whole purpose of the enterprise. Prabhu (1987:46–7) is one who takes this view, arguing that the open-ended exchange of opinions may make learners feel insecure. He favours what he calls 'reasoning-gap' activities, in which learners are given practical reasoning tasks with the security of knowing that there is a single right answer.

As with the other factors we are considering here, deciding on the right amount and type of regulation calls for some careful thought, and it can only be achieved through trying out ideas in the classroom.

▶ ## TASK 49

Look again at the two activities in Task 47, and then at the following activity. How would you assess each activity in terms of the balance between stimulating genuine discussion, and regulating the activity to guide learners in a non-threatening way? What specific techniques are used to do this?

Age and Wisdom   **Student A** You must defend the view that *"Older is not necessarily wiser, that is, that there is no direct relationship between how old someone is and how wise or intelligent he or she is."* You know that this excuse is often used for forcing youths to obey their parents (even though the children know what is better for themselves) and for forcing young employees to hold lower positions in companies than older (but not as intelligent) employees. Your partner thinks that an older person has "the voice of experience." Well, that just isn't enough nowadays.

Think of all the things that young people can teach their elders! Think of the benefits that the younger generation have compared with previous generations: technology, education, travel.... Give examples that show that *you* are right. You must not agree with your opponent. Take a few minutes to gather your thoughts on this subject.

Whenever your opponent gives an example of the strengths (mental, spiritual) that come with age, remind him or her of the tremendous weaknesses that also come.

Student B You must defend the view that *"With age comes wisdom; that is, the older a person is, the wiser, or more, intelligent he or she is."* Your opponent thinks that your idea is old-fashioned and untrue. Your partner does not see any relationship between age and wisdom.

(*Duff 1986:175*)

8.7 Process teaching in review

When learners express themselves spontaneously, they are faced with the immensely difficult task of coping with a number of competing demands under great pressure of time: being clear, relevant, an effective listener as well as a speaker, a sensitive turn-taker, and so on. In process teaching our job is to subtly regulate some of these factors so that the learner can have every chance to elaborate her grammar. But, in any one task all these factors co-exist—there will be a time limit of some kind, a topic which is more or less familiar, a measure of shared knowledge, and a number of other factors besides. Ultimately, it is their combined effect which will influence the learner's performance. We therefore need to appraise task design from a number of perspectives.

▶ TASK 50

How would you appraise the following activity? With a particular group of learners in mind, consider how you might modify it to reduce or increase the pressure which learners would be put under. You could use the checklist below.

> Talk about one of these topics. Can you keep talking for one minute?
>
> | | |
> |:---:|:---:|
> | **neighbours** | **travelling by bus** |
> | **your favourite drink(s)** | **a street you know well** |
> | **airports** | **your daily routine** |
> | **restaurants** | **brothers and sisters** |
> | **your home town** | **love** |

(*Doff and Jones 1991:32*)

Checklist

Time pressure:	How much time to plan? How much time available for the activity itself? Will the learners have more time through writing, or is the task purely an oral one?
Topic:	How familiar is the topic? How familiar (to the learner) will the development of the topic be through the task? (for example, how much scope for unpredictable interaction?)
Shared knowledge:	How much built-in regulation of shared knowledge? Will listeners have to listen for unshared information? Will speakers have to spell out certain meanings which are not self-evident?

Many teachers are experienced in making swift judgements about whether a certain activity will or will not work with their class. The suggestion here is that we make the reasons for such judgements explicit, and that we follow them through so that once the task is over, we can make a reasonable assessment about what worked, what didn't work, and why. This does not mean that teachers need to listen out for the grammatical detail of their learners' performance. It is much more a matter of making a rough assessment of the general factors which we can observe as learners work on the task: Were they evidently under too much pressure? Did they complete the task prematurely? Did they have very little to say? Did some learners look uncomfortable? In Section Three we will consider how these questions might be acted upon, with regard to some specific tasks.

The ideas examined in **8** fit into a framework which can help teachers to deploy and to appraise process tasks in a systematic and organized way. Each of the factors we have examined—the regulation of time, topic, context-gap—falls into one of three distinct stages in the performance of a task (Skehan 1994). The first is the pre-task stage, including the regulation of planning time. The second stage, the task itself, involves the regulation of time, topic, and context-gap. The third stage, the post-task activity, is something which we have not yet considered. It includes the public performance of a task which was previously undertaken in small groups. With the confidence and experience gained from working in the group, the learners then perform the task in front of the whole class. In effect, this is another way of regulating pressure, in the hope that learners will attend more carefully to the quality of their language in view of the whole-class exposure which they know it will subsequently receive. See a number of the tasks in Willis and Willis (1988).

Another form of post-task work is reflection activity, where learners explicitly consider the quality of the language they used in the main task, and reflect on possible improvements. We will examine reflection activities in **9.6**.

In summary, then:

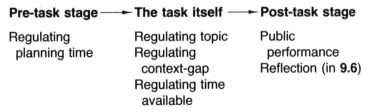

Pre-task stage ⟶ The task itself ⟶ Post-task stage

Regulating	Regulating topic	Public
planning time	Regulating	performance
	context-gap	Reflection (in **9.6**)
	Regulating time	
	available	

Figure 11

There are other ways in which process teaching can be regulated. See, for example, Brown and Yule (1983), Long and Crookes (1992), and Crookes and Gass (1993). But the outline above indicates that process tasks can, and should be, planned and evaluated as systematically as possible.

9 Teaching grammar as skill

9.1 Product, process, and the critical gap

Through a combination of product and process teaching, teachers can give their learners both a focus on specific grammatical forms and opportunities to deploy these forms in language use. The two approaches have complementary functions. In product teaching, we focus the learner's attention on forms. But, aware that much of this knowledge can remain delicate and transitory unless the learner can put it to use in a meaning-focused context, we turn to process teaching. However, as we have just seen, process teaching requires a delicate touch, and many of these forms may never emerge at all, or not at all adequately. So, we can easily find ourselves facing a kind of critical gap between process teaching and product teaching. Many features of the grammar will be lost—focused on and practised in product teaching, yet never emerging adequately in process work.

9.2 A learner focus on grammar

To deal with this, we will need an approach which allows a focus on grammatical forms, but which at the same time retains a measure of self-expression and meaning-focus. If we can achieve such a balance, then we can help guide the learner to appreciate and use grammar as a communicative device, encouraging a richer deployment of grammar in more subtly regulated process tasks. But this focus on form will have to be by, rather than for, the learner, and the attention to meaning and self-expression will have to involve the learner quite directly. This approach, then, means guiding the learner's own attention to grammar, and designing tasks which help us to teach learners the skill of using and attending to grammar in language use. It is for this reason that the approach is called 'teaching grammar as skill'. Its objectives are complementary to those of product and process teaching, as was outlined in 6.

We will look at three different ways of teaching grammar as skill. First, we consider how listening and reading activities can combine a focus on meaning with attention to grammar (9.3). Second, we consider how learners can be guided to make their own decisions about how to deploy grammar in tasks where they are provided only with words (9.4). Finally, we consider how learners can be guided to reflect more explicitly on the quality of their own grammar, and to consider ways in which it might be improved (**9.5**).

9.3 Noticing as skill

In **7.1** we examined noticing activities which focus very tightly on grammar in isolation from the ongoing flow of language use. But if we were to leave it at that, there would always be the danger that in actual contexts of use, the learner will consistently fail to notice—or re-notice— grammar, engaging instead a top-down mode of processing in which grammar can be largely disregarded. Given the importance of noticing as the gateway to subsequent learning, this would be a serious handicap. In **9.3** we consider another way of exploiting noticing, with learners required to notice grammar in order to make sense of language in context, presented through listening and reading tasks.

Listening and reading tasks furnish rich opportunities for learners to notice grammar in context, as part of the wider skill of making sense of written and spoken discourse. Let us say, for example, that we want the class to think about tense and time, and the way in which different tenses signal different time references. We could use a tape of a dialogue such as the following:

Bill: Hi Jane. How's life?
Jane: Terrible, since you ask. I didn't get that job I applied for—the one I told you about—and my cat has started eating the carpet again. Oh, and my sister Denise arrived recently and decided to stay with me without even asking if it was OK or not. I don't really like her very much, but at least we have the same taste in music, so we're both going out to a lot of concerts. I don't talk to her, though…

Of course, this text is a specially constructed one, but for a good reason. It includes a lot of time references which are signalled almost entirely through the grammar: 'I *didn't get* that job' (past), '…and my cat *has started eating*…' (recent, including and up to the present), and so on. In fact, the text has been specifically designed to ensure that it is grammar, and not lexis, which does this signalling. In other words, lexical clues such as 'I went for that job interview *yesterday*' (where 'yesterday' reinforces the past meaning) have been deliberately avoided. This makes it difficult for the learner to process the language top-down. If we want learners to attend to the grammar, and to demonstrate that they have really noticed it, then we have to construct tasks which require them to notice and to process grammar in order to complete the task successfully. This is the aim of the following task (which is based on the above dialogue about Jane and her sister).

► TASK 51

1 As you listen to the dialogue, decide whether each of the events in the list: (a) happened in the the past; (b) began in the past but is still going on; (c) is planned for the future. Put a tick in the right column.

Event	Happened and finished	Still going on	Future
Jane applies for job			
Jane gets result of her application			
Jane's cat causes problems for Jane			
Jane's sister arrives			
Jane and sister go to concerts			

2 How might you adapt the activity to make the target grammar more explicit, i.e. to vary the type of consciousness-raising? In what circumstances might you follow this up with further work on the tenses involved?

Increasingly, learners are given listening and reading tasks which encourage them to listen and read in a top-down way, formulating predictions about what the text might be about, taking bearings from the lexis, and gliding over much of the grammar: see the discussion of top-down processing in pedagogy in Cook: *Discourse*, pages 79–86. In one sense this is all to the good, because it is exactly what competent language users do: they process top-down, only giving direct attention to the grammar when all else fails. But they can only do this because much of their systemic knowledge, including knowledge about the grammar, has been automated and proceduralized. They rarely notice the grammar because they can follow its signposting more or less automatically. Learners, though, are in a different position altogether. They need to notice grammar, because if they do not, they will never learn it very effectively. The question is: how much do we make noticing grammar a necessary condition for completing the task? We can, as with the task about Jane, make it very necessary indeed.

▶ **TASK 52**

Both the listening and the reading activities below have certain grammatical forms which are prominent in the text: linking words (with the listening task) and the past and perfect tenses (with the reading task). How much does each activity require the learner to notice these forms as a necessary condition for completing it?

Activity 1

Instructions to students

Below are some pictures to show you how to make sherry trifle. The pictures are in the right order but the instructions are jumbled. Listen to the recording, work with a partner and match the pictures with the method.

Instructions to teachers

Input. Focus on the instructions. Pair work. The students could try to match the instructions to the correct picture before they hear the tape; however, the tape focuses on the use of link words to make instructions more cohesive, and this should be emphasized.

Tapescript

Method

And the method is, first slice the cake thickly. Next spread the jam on the slices and put them in the bottom of the bowl. Then put the raspberries, or another soft fruit if you prefer, on top and pour the sherry over. Now prepare the custard and leave it to cool before pouring it on top of the raspberries. Leave it until cold and the custard has set. After that whisk the cream and put it on top of the custard. Finally decorate your trifle with the almonds and cherries and put it in the fridge until you are ready to serve.

For more practice of 'cooking' verbs and utensils, see Resource Book *C1*; for practice in giving instructions in non-food contexts see Resource Book *C2, C3, C4, C5*.

☐ Pour on top.
☐ Whisk cream.
☐ Spread jam on the slices.
☐ Pour sherry on.
☐ Leave until cold and custard has set.
☐ Decorate with almonds and cherries.

☒ Slice the cake thickly.
☐ Prepare custard.
☐ Leave custard to cool.
☐ Put slices in bottom of bowl.
☐ Put on top of custard.
☐ Put raspberries on top.

(Black, McNorton, Malderez, and Parker 1986:66–7)

Activity 2

3.1 THE PAST PERFECT TENSE

Presentation

Read the passage below, which is the beginning of a novel, and answer the questions.

Julia Stretton was late. The Tartan Army had planted a bomb at Heathrow, and Julia, who had gone the long way round past the airport to avoid the usual congestion on the approach roads to the M3, had been delayed for two hours by police and army checkpoints. When she finally joined the motorway further down, she put thoughts of Paul Mason out of her mind, and concentrated on her driving. She drove quickly for an hour, breaking the speed limit all the way, and not particularly concerned about being spotted by one of the police helicopters.

She left the motorway near Basingstoke, and drove steadily down the main road towards Salisbury. The plain was grey and misty. It had been a cool, wet summer in Britain, and, although it was still only July, there had been reports of snow along the Yorkshire coast, and flooding in parts of Cornwall.

A few miles beyond Salisbury, on the road to Blandford Forum, Julia stopped at a roadside cafe for a cup of coffee, and as she sat at the plastic-topped table she had time at last for reflection.

It had been the surprise of seeing Paul Mason that had probably upset her more than anything else; that, and the way it had happened, and the place...

(Adapted from *A Dream of Wessex*)

1 In what order do you think the five events below happened?

Julia was stopped at army checkpoints.
Julia stopped for coffee.
Julia saw Paul Mason.
Julia joined the motorway.
The Tartan Army planted a bomb.

2 At which point in time does the writer choose to begin his story?

(Doff, Jones, and Mitchell 1984:21)

9.4 Teaching grammar as grammaticization

In **9.4** we consider an approach to grammar teaching where learners are given words which they combine and grammaticize in their own ways. This approach has been motivated in large part by the work of Rutherford (1987) and Widdowson (1990:79–98).

We saw in 5 that learners do not learn grammar overnight, nor do they learn it in isolation. Instead, they appear to shift gradually from words to grammar. In the early stages, learners use words with minimal grammar, as with 'aeroplane fly sky', or they deploy fixed chunks of language as if they were single words. It is only gradually that the grammar emerges, so that learners progressively learn to *grammaticize*, i.e. apply grammar to their language. This general trend—from lexis to grammar— seems to work its way out with both first and second language learning, and may even help to explain the way in which all human languages have evolved over time (Givon 1979a, 1979b).

And yet, while language learning may well follow this route, language teaching certainly does not. On the contrary, we seem to spend a great deal of our time pressing our learners to move off in the opposite direction—from grammar to lexis. In other words, we start out with a target grammatical structure and we require our learners to manipulate this structure by changing the lexical items in some way. Sometimes this is done quite explicitly, as with a formal drill, and sometimes less explicitly, but it is certainly a very marked trend in product teaching.

▶ TASK 53

Look back over some of the Tasks in 7. Where do you recognize the underlying pattern 'from grammar to lexis'?

So language learning and product teaching sometimes appear to be progressing in quite different directions: the learner gradually reaches out for grammar from a secure basis in words, while the materials writer starts from a basis in target grammar and encourages the learner to reach out for different lexical items as she manipulates the grammar. Of course, it would be unreasonable to say that all target language tasks are like this, but the general pattern is clear enough. Why not, then, simply reverse the pattern? Instead of giving learners fully formed grammatical items, give them words instead, and get them to do the grammaticizing for themselves. This sounds straightforward enough, so as a first attempt consider the following:

Here are four words. Order them, and add the grammar:

arrive   Jane   leave   John

What might the learner make of this exercise? She could come up with something like 'Jane arrive. John leave', or, just as plausibly, 'John arrive. Jane leave', and decide to leave it at that. After all, it is clear what's going on here: one does the arriving, and the other does the leaving. Why bother with any further grammatical elaboration at all? In this exercise learners are given no reason to use grammar, and no indication of what kind of grammar they might use if they wished to.

But we know that many learners use grammar only to the extent that it helps to make their meaning clear, and some learners will remain with a fossilized system if that appears to be communicatively adequate. In the exercise above, we are asking learners to pluck grammar out of a contextual void, with no obvious purpose in mind. We need to give them a purpose, motivating a communicative deployment of grammar to clarify meaning. This is the aim of the following exercise:

Here are four words. Choose one of the situations below and then decide how you will put these words together using grammar:

arrive   *Jane*   *leave*   *John*

Situation 1: You know that John doesn't like Jane.
Situation 2: John and Jane are good friends, but Jane is feeling ill.

This is a quite different kind of exercise. The learner is given a choice between two contexts, and has to grammaticize according to the context she chooses. Her grammaticization will vary depending on her choice. She will produce either something like 'Jane arrived and so John left' (for Situation 1) or 'John arrived but Jane had to leave' (for Situation 2). What we have here is the skeleton of a grammaticization task which keys in with the learning process in two important respects. Firstly, the direction of processing is from lexis to grammar: grammar emerges as the product of the learner's choices, rather than being injected into the classroom as the product of the syllabus designer's selection of target language. Secondly, the learner is grammaticizing in the very act of making her meaning clear, in a way which resembles the process of language use.

Yet the learner is not given a completely free hand in the choices she can make. We will want to direct her down certain paths, creating a need to signal particular forms and meanings. To do this effectively we will have to choose our words and our contexts with some care. In the exercise above, it is the linking of clauses to signal cause and effect which we are after: 'Jane arrived and *so* . . .'.

▶ TASK 54

What kinds of situations could you give learners in the following exercise, in order to encourage the use of grammar to signal (1) contrast (*but, however,* etc.) and (2) cause/effect?

[*Jane   live   countryside]* – *[she   work   city]*

Situation 1:
Situation 2:

Now we are in a position to expand on these principles, fashioning a grammaticization task with choices being made across a whole text. This is the purpose of the following task.

Look at these three pictures. They are part of a story about Tom, and they could be the beginning, the middle, or the end of the story. Use the pictures and the words below to make up your own version of Tom's story. Use all the words and parts of words provided (but in any order you like), and add grammar and any other words you want to make your story as clear as possible.

(Pictures from *Ur 1988:216*)

Tom	[live – language teacher – London]
it	[look for – binoculars – boat]
he	[be – very miserable]
	[stop – pick up]
-ed	[live – desert island]
was	[distance – boat – see]
used to	

1 In pairs, write down the outline of your story.
2 Tell your story to the rest of the class. When you are listening to other people's stories, make notes on how they differ from your own version.

In this way, learners work with a kind of unfocused context, with the pictures and the words sketching out the briefest outline of a plot. How the plot develops is up to them. They will determine exactly what happens and when, and how the discourse will resolve itself: whether things turn out well or tragically for Tom. Here are two (equally plausible) grammaticized versions of Tom's story:

Version 1
Tom used to work in London as a language teacher. Now he's living unhappily on a desert island. Every day he looks out for boats through his binoculars. Last week he actually saw a boat far off in the distance, but unfortunately it didn't stop to pick him up. Tom is a very miserable man.

Version 2
Tom used to live on a desert island, and he was very miserable. Every day he used to look through his binoculars for boats. Last week he finally saw a boat in the distance, and it stopped and picked him up. Now Tom works in London as a language teacher. Lucky Tom.

▶   **TASK 55**

1 Imagine that you have given the above task to one of your classes. Which of the following grammar points are they most— and least—likely to use?
   – prepositions of place
   – tense to distinguish different time references
   – conditionals
   – grammar words used to refer to people and objects
   – clauses to signal contrast or cause and effect

2 The original and full set of pictures is reproduced in Figure 9 (**8.1**). Why were only three pictures used in the version above?

The learners' task, then, is to formulate their own interpretation of the story, and in so doing to make this interpretation clear to everyone else. Grammaticization tasks exploit the notion of context-gap which was discussed in **8.5**. The learners have to attend both to meaning and form. This kind of guided language use is what we want to encourage when we teach grammar as skill. If we wanted to increase the degree of choice, widening the context-gap, then we could give fewer cueing words than in the task above. Alternatively, we could provide an unsequenced list of words, so that there is no obvious indication of how they might be combined. To increase the pressure, we could make the whole activity an oral one, and reduce the available planning time.

▶ # TASK 56

1 How would you use the pictures below to construct a grammaticization task? Think about the meanings which the story is
likely to involve. For example, there are a number of actions
which have a clear purpose leading, perhaps, to the signalling
of causation. Similarly, some events seem to occur in sequence
(*and/then*) while others may have occurred at the same time as
each other (*while/as*). What other features of the plot strike you
as significant?

(*Soars and Soars 1988:14*)

2 What changes would you make with the words and pictures to
vary the degree of guidance?

Grammaticization tasks can also be used to stimulate and guide interaction in conversation, though here we cannot give learners the same clear
lexical framework because this might constrain their flexibility and spon-
taneity. Nevertheless, there are cases where, particularly at lower levels,
such tasks can have a liberating effect, particularly in comparison with
more controlled, product-oriented activities. For example, we saw in **7.2**
how learners are sometimes given fixed expressions and dialogues to
practise and rehearse, with little scope for making their own decisions
about how the language can be formulated.

▶ # TASK 57

To what extent does the following task encourage learners to make
their own choices? How would you increase (or decrease) the scope
for choice?

Set 3   Places: location (2)

record shop	travel agent's	flower shop
bank	shoe shop	Odeon cinema
video shop	wine bar	book shop
newsagent's	post office	café
chemist's	pizza bar	

Record Shop	Bank		
Video Shop	News-agent's		
Chemist's		Travel Agent's		Shoe Shop	Wine Bar	
Post Office		Pizza Bar		Flower Shop	Odeon Cinema	
		Book Shop		Café	

1. **Talk about the places on the plan, like this:**

   There's a record shop.

   There's a . . .

2.   Is there a bank near here?

        Yes. There's one next to the newsagent's.

Ask for these places in the shopping centre. Answer with next to.

a record shop	a video shop	a cinema
a wine bar	a newsagent's	a café
a book shop	a shoe shop	

3.   Is there a chemist's near here?

        Yes. There's one opposite the post office.

Ask for these places. Answer with opposite.

a record shop	a flower shop	a travel agent's	a wine bar
a cinema	a book shop	a post office	a pizza bar

4.   Where can I buy a film?

        At the chemist's.

        Turn left at the pizza bar and it's on your

        right.

You are outside the cinema. Ask where you can buy the following. Answer giving directions.

a newspaper	a book about London
a cassette	a cup of tea and a sandwich

5. **Look at the dialogue and the plan again. Work in pairs. One of you is a stranger and one of you lives in the town. You are outside the cinema. You want a record shop and you want to get some stamps. Write out the conversations afterwards.**

(*Abbs and Freebairn 1982:47*)

This kind of procedure has its merits, but a proliferation of these activities could block out any genuinely active engagement by the learner. They are likely to approach the activity in Task 57 with a well-developed schematic knowledge about location, shops, and asking for directions. What they will not know is the precise ways in which these meanings are encoded in the target language.

We could reformulate this activity so that learners are required to make full use of what they already know (their schematic knowledge). The teacher could begin by introducing the broad context—a stranger in town needing to make some purchases—and then present just those key words with which the learners are not already familiar. The rest is left to the learners' familiarity with the general context involved (their existing schematic knowledge), as they embark on the following task:

Student A: You want to find a post office and a bookshop. Find out from your partner where to go. Use the following words, and add any other words you like:

> *where . . .?*
> *post*
> *buy*
> *near here*
> *letter*

Student B: Give directions to your partner using the map provided. Use the following words, and add any other words you like:

> *left*
> *right*
> *turn*
> *next to*
> *opposite*

Again, the teacher has considerable flexibility in determining how much guidance to give. More or fewer cue words could be given, though exactly which words to provide would depend in part on the learners' existing vocabulary. Of course, this task will not generate the kind of well-formed language provided in the original version. Instead, it will reveal what the learners already know, and what they themselves are capable of. Having brought them this far, the teacher is now well placed to fashion some of the language the learners have been working with, demonstrating, for instance, how 'Where I buy book?' can be reshaped into 'Where can I buy a book?'. Another oral grammaticization task is outlined in **14.2** (Task 81).

The great advantage of this approach is that the learners are now reshaping and improving their own language, with a greater sense of involvement in the whole procedure. In effect, grammaticization tasks lead to another kind of activity which is part of the teaching of grammar as skill—those in which learners reflect on the quality of their own language, and it is reflection which we now move on to consider.

9.5 Reflection

In teaching grammar as skill, we are aiming to encourage greater attention to grammar in meaning-focused work. The difficulty with process tasks, as we saw, is that the teacher has of necessity only a very indirect influence on the quality of learners' language. It may be that the learners have been made more conscious of shortcomings in their language. But then again, they may not. We know that grammar has been an important objective of the task, but what have our learners made of it all? To some learners, it is possible that all this flurry of process work means very little. When the dust has settled, they may shrug their shoulders in puzzled amazement: 'Why did the teacher make us do that? Why didn't she *teach* us anything today?'

One solution is to encourage learners to reflect on the quality of the language they are using, appraising its strengths and its weaknesses for themselves. There is every chance that they will be motivated to do so, precisely because it is their language, and as such it should be more salient and significant than language injected directly from the syllabus. Furthermore, through reflection activities we are implicitly providing a rationale for process teaching. Once a process task is over, teachers and learners meet in explicit consideration of the language used, and the purpose in using it. As has already been suggested, reflection activities constitute a kind of post-task stage which fits into a wider framework of task activity (see Figure 11 on page 97).

▶ ## TASK 58

The activity below follows on from a task in which learners tape-recorded a story of their own choosing. What skills and qualities do learners need for this kind of reflection to work well?

> *Tense/Hesitation devices*
>
> Choose about a minute of your recorded story and listen to it again as follows.
>
> *First listening*   One of you should listen for the verb tenses and the other should listen for vocabulary items. Write down anything which you think was an error or could have been done better. Discuss your notes with your partner and decide how it could have been said better. Ask your teacher to help you if necessary.
>
> *Second listening*   As you listen see if you can notice any of the things that make continuous speech sound more natural, for example:
> hesitation noises such as *erm, mmm, err*
> introductory phrases such as *well, so then, anyway, oh*
> things which involve the listener in the story such as
> *so,   you see,   you know,   do you see what I mean?*

(Nolasco 1987:58)

A reflection stage will help us to lead learners to critically reflect on their grammar, comparing what they actually said with what they might have said. This, then, is the theory. But there are practical constraints. For some learners, all this critical reflection may just add to the pressure. 'It's bad enough that we are asked to express ourselves in such a public way', they might reason, 'but then to have our language subjected to critical scrutiny by all and sundry...' Once again, we encounter the difficulties posed by pressure: learners will only commit themselves to a task if they feel motivated, but they are unlikely to throw themselves into an activity if they have real doubts or fears about their own role in it. Somehow, then, we need to lead learners gently into self- and peer-appraisal, perhaps through tasks which encourage them to look critically at language without feeling that their own efforts are being singled out for critical attention.

► TASK 59

How do the following activities seek to achieve this aim? What other ways can you think of to accomplish the same objective?

Activity 1

GRAMMAR:	Patterns proposed by the students
LEVEL:	Post-beginner and beyond
TIME:	20 minutes
MATERIALS:	None

1 Ask the students to work on their own and write down five sentences they *know* are wrong but that feel right to them.

2 Now ask them to rewrite five sentences they know are correct English but which all the same *feel* wrong to them.

3 Ask the students to read out some of the sentences from both categories and explain why they feel the way they do. For many people this is a novel and curious linguistic awareness activity.

4 To help students deepen their awareness of feelings of grammatical rightness and wrongness in the target language, have two envelopes pinned up in your classroom, one marked:
   Right that feel(s) wrong
   and the other marked:
   Wrong that feel(s) right
   Invite students to put new sentences they find that fit either category into the appropriate envelope.
   Every now and then ask the class to look at the sentences so collected and discuss them.

(*Rinvolucri 1984:95*)

Activity 2

Editing a text:
Doing your own corrections

Every writer has to learn to check written work. Using what
you have learned in this unit (and in any other course), study
the following passage about horses and cows, correcting it as
necessary:

> Horses are useful animals, but they are not more usefull than
> cow. It is easier to ride horse than cow, but it is easier to
> milk a cow than horse. Cows are generally regarded as
> female, and the male get the special name 'bull' to show that
> he is not female. Horses, however, are generally regarded
> male, the female getting the special name mare to show that
> she is not male. We can, however, call male horse 'Stallion',
> but there is no special name, in english language at least, for
> female cow.

(McArthur 1984:28)

Once having introduced reflection in a relatively non-threatening context,
we can move on to organize reflection tasks which deal directly with the
learner's own language. But this does not mean that we need relinquish
all control over the forms which the learner will focus on. Whereas the
activity in Task 58 depends heavily on the forms the learners happen to
produce, other activities will involve more careful guidance. For example,
we can design tasks which focus very explicitly on, say, ways in which
the learners' first language interferes with their production in the target
language. As we saw in **5.2**, learners typically make a great many errors
by applying features of the L1 to their performance in the target language.

▶   TASK 60

The following extract outlines a procedure for teachers to raise learner awareness of factors encountered in translating between the first language and English. What kind of guidance is to be provided in the reflection stage of the procedure (stage 3)?

5.6 Variations on a theme: reverse translation

PREPARATION

1 Choose two passages of ten to fifteen lines, one in English and one in the mother tongue. The text should preferably be self-contained, that is, easy to understand even out of context.

2 Prepare a task sheet for each passage and make copies for half the class.

IN CLASS

1 Divide the class into two even groups, A and B. Give Group A task sheet A, Group B, task sheet B. Out of class, the students translate their respective texts. Group A from English into L1, Group B from L1 into English.

2 Each student chooses a partner from the opposite group. They exchange translations but not original texts. Their task is to translate the translation they have been given, either back into English (Group B) or back into L1 (Group A).

The students should do the reverse translation alone, without discussion or consultation. It could even be done out of class, but interest will be greater if the writing is done on the spot. A strict time-limit of 20 minutes should be set.

3 Next, ask each student to rejoin his or her partner, and:

a. Discuss any difficulties they have had. They should refer only to the translations, not to the original text.
b. Read through each other's work.
c. Exchange the original texts and compare them with the reverse translation.

(Duff 1989:147)

As well as being face-threatening, paying careful attention to one's own language production is a skilled business, particularly for learners who are not experienced in this kind of work, or who are by nature more interested in getting their meanings over than in scrutinizing the language they use to do so. Learners, therefore, may well require some careful guidance in the skill of critical language study.

► ## TASK 61

Here is an extract from a book entitled *Learning to Learn English*. What particular skills are the authors seeking to develop here? How explicit are they, i.e. is this a kind of consciousness-raising exercise? What additional key questions might you wish to give your learners?

---

1   Points to assess

Before you can assess your use of grammar, you need to be clear about what exactly you want to assess.

a) First of all you need to consider what kinds of grammatical mistakes you think are serious. Some are more serious than others because they make the meaning unclear and can cause confusion. Look at the examples of spoken English below. In each one there is a sentence (marked *) with a mistake. Decide how serious you think each mistake is and why. Discuss.

  i)   A: What does your brother do?
       B: *He work in a factory.

  ii) *Where you go for your holiday?

  iii) A: What's the matter?
       B: *I've been cutting my finger.

  iv) A: Are you going swimming?
       B: *It depends from the weather.

  v)   *What means 'flabbergasted'?

b) Do you think it is more important to be correct when writing or when speaking? Why?

c) When you have thought about which mistakes are serious and whether you are going to assess your speaking or writing, you can choose particular points to assess. Here are some suggestions:
   – tenses, e.g. past tenses, present tenses
   – prepositions e.g. of direction, of location
   – question tags e.g. It's a nice day, *isn't it?*
   – word order
   – comparatives e.g. She's *taller* than Fred.
   – superlatives e.g. She's *the tallest* in the class.
   etc.
   Select only two or three of these at a time.

(*Ellis and Sinclair 1989:48–9*)

We may want to lead learners into the art of reflection step by step, with a gradual shift away from the controlled evaluation of someone else's language, as with Activity 2 in Task 59, through to the point where they feel both happy and able to assess their own and each others' oral production. We should stop short, though, of requiring them simultaneously to both communicate freely and attend carefully to the quality of their output. This would amount to sabotage, and anyway demands a level of mental gymnastics which no language user could reasonably be expected to have. Imagine coming to the end of an involving discussion, only to be asked 'How exactly did you put that point you made about TV being bad for children?'. The more involved you were with your message, the less likely it is that you will have any recollection at all about its precise linguistic packaging.

▶ ## TASK 62

Imagine that you give your learners a role-play activity. Listed below are four options for language reflection which could be attached to the activity. How would you assess and grade each option in terms of the degree of guidance and control which it offers? What kind of listening is required with each option?

Option 1
After you have finished your dialogue, try to remember some of the things you said. How did you put some of the points you made? How well do you think you expressed them?

Option 2
Record your dialogue. When you have finished, listen again to what was said and discuss the language you used. Which points are you happy with, and which do you think you could improve? Think particularly about the expressions you used to persuade the other person to do something.

Option 3
Before you start your dialogue, work with your partner and make brief notes of what each of you might say. Check your plan with the teacher, then pass it over to another pair of students, who will listen carefully as you act out the scene. Afterwards, discuss and compare what you planned with what you actually said.

Option 4
Work in groups of four. As one pair acts out the role-play the other pair listens out for how verbs are used. When both pairs have finished, discuss together what you did well and what you would like to improve. Report your summary to the rest of the class and the teacher.

Motivating and educating learners to operate in this way can have a very positive impact on the learning process. The learner is able to tune in to her own language, a skill which she may then carry with her beyond the confines of the classroom. At the same time, a single reflection task might require attention to a wide range of language forms, each one occurring in the learner's own discourse. This is a far cry from the narrow language focus typical of much product teaching. Learners do not learn grammar on a conveyor belt system, systematically noticing and instantly structuring each grammatical form as it swings briefly into view. They need to keep re-noticing. Teaching grammar as skill, we can offer them rich and recurring opportunities to re-notice and restructure their hypotheses about language. See O'Malley and Chamot (1990) for a discussion of the importance of this kind of self-awareness in the learning process.

10 Conclusions

What is grammar? There is more than one answer to this question, as we have seen. What grammar is depends on how you choose to look at it, so that we can regard it as a formal mechanism, as a functional system for signalling meanings, or as a dynamic resource which both users and learners call on in different ways at different times.

Yet whatever our perspective, it is apparent—and important—that grammar does not exist in a void. In language description, we have seen that the more precisely we wish to formulate statements about form and meaning, the more we are compelled to acknowledge the interdependency between grammar, lexis, and context (see the discussion in 2). Similarly, in language learning there is no obvious boundary between grammar and lexis: learners may represent much of their linguistic knowledge in lexical terms—as formulaic chunks or as partially fixed routines—so that what may look like grammar to the outside observer may be thought of as largely lexical by the learner (see 5). In language use it is clear that grammar is closely tied to discourse, acting as a resource to be activated to different degrees and in different ways depending on the context (see 4). In short, grammar is a dependent, rather than an independent, phenomenon.

Having an understanding of these issues is important for language teaching, where no single or narrow conception of grammar will do. Learners themselves have a multiplicity of needs: they require some sense of the regularity in the language system, they need some understanding of the relationship between forms and functions, and they need an ability to act on this knowledge in language use. But learning to deal with these needs takes time, because language learning is a gradual process. Effective grammar teaching means being aware of these different needs, and having the resources at our disposal for meeting them. This will require a variety of teaching strategies and approaches, ranging from the careful control of grammar (as product) through to the more subtle shaping of process tasks. Ultimately, the teaching of grammar (like the beast itself) is multi-dimensional. In order to put these different approaches into practice, we have to detach ourselves from any one perspective on grammar, and therefore from any one inflexible teaching method.

Exploring grammar

Section Three is devoted to an exploration through classroom investigation of some of the ideas which have been put forward in Sections One and Two. As we revisit the major themes of Section Two—grammar as product, as process, and as skill—suggestions are made for implementing and appraising these ideas, bearing in mind that appraisal is as important as implementation. There are two main objectives. One is to try out classroom activities which are based on some of the principles we have discussed. The other is to use these activities as a basis for subsequent classroom activity, making working judgements about their effectiveness, and considering how and why changes might be made in future work.

▶   **TASK 63**

Aim

To consider the approach, or approaches, taken to the teaching of grammar in the materials you work with.

Resources

Textbooks, syllabus, and any additional materials you use.

Procedure

Make a critical assessment of the materials you teach with, considering which perspective on grammar is predominant. The following checklist may be useful:

Grammar as product
- How much emphasis is there on form, or on meaning?
- How idealized, or how context-sensitive, are the generalizations which learners are given about grammar?
- Are there any noticing activities?
- How much support is provided for the learner, and how much emphasis on self-discovery by the learner?

Grammar as process
- How much opportunity, in general, is there for language use?
- If there are opportunities for language use, what approach is taken to factors such as time pressure, preparation time, the regulation of shared knowledge, and to familiarity with the topics involved?

Grammar as skill
- Are learners involved in reflection activities of any kind?
- In listening and reading activities, is attention to grammar actually necessary for the tasks to be completed?

Evaluation

In which areas are these materials least satisfactory to you? Can you identify specific aspects to grammar teaching which you would be interested in developing, either through your own materials or, where possible, through drawing on alternative published material?

12 Exploring grammar as product

12.1 Exploring noticing

▶ TASK 64

Aim
To design noticing tasks for a particular grammatical form, or forms, at two different levels of idealization, and to assess the effectiveness of these tasks for learners.

Resources
The discussion in 2 and 7.1.

Procedure
1 Choose a grammatical construction which is suitable for a particular group of your learners. Formulate a broad (grammar at 30 000 feet) idealization about this form and the meaning which it is typically used to signal. For instance, the formal idealization about tense shifting for reported speech illustrated in 3.3 after Task 12.

2 Design two noticing activities for the form you have chosen. One of the tasks should be relatively explicit and guided, i.e. *for* the learner, the other more implicit, leaving more to be done *by* the learner. Use the example activities in 7.1 as a guide.

3 Give both activities to a group of learners, perhaps by dividing a class into two, giving one half the explicit task, and vice versa. Make sure that you do this in advance of any more productive work on the form in question, i.e. before the learners have done structuring activities. Where feasible, explain that these activities are designed simply to make them think about an aspect of grammar.

Evaluation
1 Soon after the activity is over, ask a number of learners to tell you about the form on which it focused. You could ask learners to put their observations down on paper.

2 To be effective, this experiment should be repeated with the distribution of task-types reversed, i.e. those who previously had the more explicit task now work on a more implicit one. Compare your findings from the two sessions. Was one task-type evidently more effective than another? Did it appear to depend on the learner in question? This kind of information will help you in doing subsequent work on noticing.

▶ **TASK 65**

Aim
As with Task 64.

Procedure
As with Task 64, but this time choose an idealization which is more finely tuned. For example, with reported speech you could choose to focus on the way in which the choice of tense varies to signal a writer's point of view, as illustrated in the text preceding Task 12.

Evaluation
As with Task 64.

12.2 Exploring structuring: choice

▶ **TASK 66**

Aim
To give learners a degree of guided choice in the forms they use in structuring activities, and to appraise the results.

Resources
The discussion in 7.3, and particularly the demonstration of choice in Task 34.

Procedure
Choose two or three forms which you will focus on in the activity, as the activity in Task 34 focuses on past, present progressive, and future passive forms. Design an activity which requires the learners to attend to choices made as a condition for completing the activity successfully. Make this condition explicit to the learners when you try it out in class. If appropriate, you could try modifying the activity illustrated in Task 35, ensuring that the choice of location, and the language used to signal it, is decided on by the learners. Alternatively, you could use the activity demonstrated in Task 34.

Evaluation
Observe how learners tackle the task. In particular, if the procedure and choice is quite new to them, they might have some difficulty understanding what is required. Note how they cope, how involved and interested they appear to be, and how successfully they manage the activity as a whole. What changes might you make in using a similar activity in the future? Did anything happen which alerted you to a difficulty in the actual design of the activity?

► TASK 67

Aim
To design a classroom activity which focuses on the choice of reference words to account for shared knowledge. To elicit learners' response to the activity.

Resources
The discussion in 7.3.

Procedure
Look back over the discussion in 7.3, and particularly Activities 1 and 2 in Task 36. Design an activity along similar lines to one of these.

Evaluation
1 This activity deliberately exploits the principle of consciousness-raising so that there is no explicit summary of the principles underlying the use of reference words. Soon after the activity is over, ask the class to say briefly what they thought its purpose was. This could be done individually, or you could have learners working collaboratively in groups. Judging from their response, how effective was the activity in creating conditions for self-discovery?

2 If the result was confusion rather than enlightenment, this may be because the learners were unfamiliar with this type of activity. Repeat the procedure, focusing on another aspect of grammar and choice, and comparing the results with what happened the first time.

► TASK 68

Aim
To design an activity focusing on social distance and to evaluate the results of its use in class.

Resources
The discussion in 3, 4.6, and 7.3.

Procedure
Look again at the activity outlined in Task 37. Use this format as a basis for constructing a similar task which focuses on politeness in social distance, and in particular on how past and present forms convey degrees of deference and attention to a person's 'face'. You could, for example, construct a dialogue involving a number of participants, each having a more or less formal relationship with the others, so that both past and present forms get used throughout the discourse. Construct a task which requires the learner to attend to these forms in order to work out the type of social relationship being signalled.

Evaluation
As with Task 67.

13 Exploring grammar as process

Here, we concentrate on investigating process teaching. Most of the factors we considered in 8 are examined, but rarely in isolation. As we have already noted (see Figure 11 on page 97), regulating process work will often fall into three distinct stages. So, wherever possible, we will consider process teaching from this wider perspective.

13.1 Exploring familiarity and preparation time

▶ TASK 69

Aim
To investigate the effects on learners' grammar of introducing unexpected elements into a planned dialogue.

Resources
The discussion in 8.3.

Procedure
Plan how you might use the activity in Task 42, or a similar activity appropriate to your class. Consider carefully what kind of modification you will introduce during the learners' performances, and at which point you will introduce it: if you introduce the change early on in the dialogue, this is likely to require more adjustment and improvisation by learners than if it occurs later. Try to make sure that the change you make will affect both participants in the dialogue, requiring some unexpected negotiation.

Evaluation
What effect did the unexpected change seem to have on the learners' language? If it was too disruptive, consider trying out a similar activity in which, for example, the change occurs later, requiring less rethinking. Where feasible, ask learners themselves to discuss and report to you their reaction to the task.

▶ TASK 70

Aim
As with Task 69.

Resources
The discussion in **8.3** and **9.5**, plus what you have learned from implementing Task 69.

Procedure
As with Task 69, but add in a reflection stage. This might involve learners working in groups of three, with the third member specifically instructed to listen out for the language which is used once the change is introduced. Be careful not to make this learner's role too demanding—see the discussion in **9.5**.

Evaluation
Ask the group of three to consider how effectively they handled the task, with the third member feeding back to the other two. Again, this reflection work will require some careful guidance when first introduced. You could monitor this procedure, assessing for yourself the learners' responses and their implications.

13.2 Investigating shared knowledge

▶ TASK 71

Aim
To investigate the effects on learners' grammar of regulating shared knowledge.

Resources
The discussion in **8.5**.

Procedure
1 Try out two different kinds of picture story with your learners: one which tells a story where the events and their sequence is self-evident . (where there will be considerable shared knowledge from the outset), and another where there is considerable ambiguity (as there is, for example, with Activity 2 in Task 45).

2 Plan how you will ask learners to produce narratives based on each of the two picture stories. Try to make the procedure as similar as possible in each case, so that whatever learners say (or write) is more likely to be due to the difference in shared knowledge than to some other factor which you have varied between the two activities. Make sure that the learners are addressing an audience (reader or listener) so that they have some reason for making their ideas clear.

Evaluation
What differences did you observe in the learners' use of grammar between the two types of story? Is there evidence that they used more grammar, or more elaborate grammar, in the case of the ambiguous story? If not, could this be because the activity was too taxing, or too unclear? What did the learners themselves make of the two experiences?

▶ **TASK 72**

Aim
To follow up Task 71, adding in regulation of preparation time.

Resources
The discussion in 8.5, together with insights gained from Task 71.

Procedure
Repeat the procedure in Task 71 but with different pictures, this time making adjustments which take into account your evaluation of Task 71.

1 If the ambiguous story proved to be too demanding, allow learners more time to prepare and plan it next time round.

2 If you felt that the ambiguous story was not demanding enough, and that it failed to stretch the learners' grammar sufficiently, select a new context which will be less familiar and more involved, requiring more inference before it can be made sense of.

Evaluation
As with Task 71.

▶ **TASK 73**

Aim
To give learners a motivation for being very clear with the language they use in a context where shared knowledge cannot be assumed, and to combine this with regulation of preparation time and reflection.

Resources
The discussion in 8.5.

Procedure
1 Look again at Activity 1 in Task 45, which creates a context in which learners have to make their meanings very clear. Think of a context for using a similar kind of activity. For example, a picture of a traffic accident which learners have to describe precisely, as if they were making an emergency telephone call to the police or the ambulance services. Or ask them to produce written instructions for a friend who is unfamiliar with the locality, describing exactly how to reach their house. Consider carefully the context you set up, identifying the particular meanings which the learners are likely to express.

2 Allow some time for preparation, but ensure that the learners who have to receive this information are not involved in its preparation, so that there is a genuine absence of shared knowledge when the activity commences. The activity could be done in pairs.

Evaluation
When the activity is over, ask each pair to consider how effectively they thought they dealt with the problem. In particular, ask the learners who had to receive the information how clear it was to them, and how the language might have been made more precise, particularly with reference to grammar.

▶ **TASK 74**

Aim
To encourage learners to use grammar for reasoning, and to investigate the effects of different features of task design.

Resources
The discussion in **8.6.**

Procedure
Take a series of pictures which require reasoning, such as the sequence illustrated in Task 48. Ask the learners to write a narrative based on the pictures, but divide the class in two and give each half a slightly different task. For example, one group has the pictures in a fixed sequence, the other does not. Or, one group has all the pictures, another has only a selection.

Evaluation
Did one group seem to produce richer examples of 'grammar for reasoning' than the other? Which group was it, and how would you explain the result you got?

▶ TASK 75

Aim

To implement and assess a task which combines regulation of shared knowledge with careful planning and opportunities for learners to reflect about grammar during the task itself.

Resources

The discussion in 8.

Procedure

1 Choose a grammatical form which you know your learners know something about, but with which they are not completely familiar.

2 Put the learners in groups and give them a kind of noticing activity, in which there are, say, ten sentences. Every sentence involves the form you have chosen; some are grammatical, others are not.

3 Ask the learners to consider the examples, identify the form being focused on, and collaborate on deciding which examples are correct and why.

4 Once the activity is in progress, tell them that they will have to formulate a clear statement of how this form is structured, and the meaning which it signals. This statement will be presented publicly to the rest of the class.

5 As they near the end of their deliberations, nominate a confident learner in each group to report their findings to the whole class.

6 During the final public presentations, observe how closely each group attends to the presentations made.

Evaluation

This activity mixes a number of factors in task regulation. It builds in a need to share knowledge of a form about which (if your judgement was right) nobody was completely informed at the outset. It builds up a degree of motivation for an accurate and clear use of language through the need for a public presentation. It encourages reflection about grammar, and it balances this pressure against considerable preparation time. How motivated and involved were the learners? Was the pressure of public presentation too great?

This type of activity could be repeated, allowing you to make changes (to pressure, preparation time) according to your findings. You might switch the topic next time, so that the groups are working with a problem or puzzle which is not directly concerned with grammar.

14   Exploring grammar as skill

14.1 Exploring noticing as skill

► TASK 76

Aim
To sensitize learners to the importance of attending to grammar to make
sense of language.

Resources
The discussion in **4.4**.

Procedure
Give the class the transcript of a garbled message transmitted over a poor
phone line, such as the text about John preceding Task 19. Working in
groups, ask them to try to reconstruct the original message by supplying
the missing words and grammar.

Evaluation
Encourage the whole class to consider carefully what they produce. In
cases where their reworked message is still not clear, point this out, asking
them to think of improvements. Accept nothing which is at all imprecise.
Finally, ask the learners what the activity tells them about the value of
grammar.

▶ TASK 77

Aim
To construct a task for noticing grammar through reading or listening.

Resources
The discussion in **9.3** and the activity in Task 51.

Procedure
Look carefully at the following passages (A, B, C), which demonstrate three different time references signalled through the present continuous. Using the activity in Task 51 as a guide, design an activity using these texts for a listening or reading task. The activity should require the learners to attend to this form in order to show they have understood the time references involved.

A	B	C
... And now the Royal Coach is turning into Parliament Square. There are thousands of people waiting in the Square, and everyone is standing on tiptoe, trying to catch a glimpse of the Royal Family. The children are all waving their Union Jacks ... Now the coach is stopping and the Queen is getting out. She's wearing ...	... There are two continuing reasons for the danger of flooding. These are that London is slowly sinking and that the tides in general are rising. Not only is central London sinking on its bed of clay, but over the centuries Britain itself is tilting. Scotland and the northwest are rising, and southeastern England is gradually dipping at a rate of one foot every hundred years ...	Having a lovely time in London. We're eating in some very expensive restaurants, and meeting lots of interesting people. I'm spending most of my time walking around central London and visiting museums. The Cup Final's tomorrow, so everyone's talking about football ...

(Doff, Jones, and Mitchell 1983:37)

Evaluation
How easy or difficult did learners appear to find the activity? How would you vary the difficulty of a similar activity in the future? How much more, if any, explicit reflection work might you do about the present progressive at this point? It might be interesting to delay any immediate follow-up work, perhaps recalling the activity a week later and asking learners what they remember of it, and what observations they made about grammar through doing the activity.

► TASK 78

Aim
To design the text and task for a noticing activity.

Resources
The discussion in **9.3**.

Procedure
Construct a noticing activity which focuses on a clear distinction in meaning signalled through grammar. Remember that the text should not provide learners with obvious lexical clues.

Evaluation
As with Task 77.

14.2 Exploring grammar as grammaticization

► TASK 79

Aim
To implement and evaluate the grammaticization activity referred to in Task 55, varying the degree of guidance.

Resources
The discussion in **9.4**.

Procedure
1 Design two versions of this activity, where one provides greater choice than the other. Consider, for instance, constructing a less controlled task where fewer words are provided, or where the words provided are arranged more loosely, and not within the fixed sentence parameters of the original version.
2 Divide the class into two or, where possible, split your two activities between two separate classes which are at the same level.

Evaluation
What differences did you note in learners' grammar between the two activities? Depending on the results, do you now think that you should make any subsequent grammaticization activities more or less guided? As with Task 76, make a point of encouraging learners to reflect on the clarity of their final versions; point out, where they have not done so themselves, any ambiguities which could be clarified through grammar.

▶ TASK 80

Aim
To experiment with adapting existing activities ('from grammar to lexis'), converting them into grammaticization activities ('from lexis to grammar'), with a focus on morphology.

Resources
The discussion in **9.4** and the activity below.

Procedure
In the activity illustrated below the learners have to choose the appropriate form for the key word by referring to a text which is already grammaticized. Plan a reworking of this activity which requires learners to construct their own grammaticization through controlled choice.

Complete the sentences

The words in capitals at the end of each sentence can be used to form a word that fits suitably into the blank space. Look at the example first.

The contestants protested about the judges' .... unfairness .... FAIR
The audience expressed their .... by booing and whistling. APPROVE
Marks will be deducted in the exam for grammatical .... ACCURATE
She frowned at them to show her .... PLEASE
The father was imprisoned for his .... to the children. CRUEL
The dog was beaten by its owner for its .... OBEY
I can't predict the results of the election with any .... CERTAIN
After our .... we are no longer on speaking terms. AGREE
We wish to apologise to passengers for any .... caused by the strike. CONVENIENT
The children held each other tight for .... WARM
I'm sorry about the .... of my desk. TIDY

(*Jones 1985:67*)

You might consider trying out an activity along the following lines:

contestant judge protest: FAIR

Evaluation
As with Task 79.

► TASK 81

Aim
To design a grammaticization activity for spoken interaction.

Resources
The discussion in **9.4** and the pictures below.

Procedure
1 Using the activity and procedure outlined at the end of **9.4** as a guide, design a grammaticization activity which is based on the pictures below.

(*Doff and Jones 1991:28–9*)

2 Note that for many learners, the context provided will already be familiar to them, i.e. it will be part of their schematic knowledge, so that they should be able to achieve quite a lot by working with a few key words. You could choose only some of the pictures, number them, and design an activity where students produce a dialogue in pairs based around, say, just two or three of the pictures, with the rest of the class having to say which pictures are being acted out.

Evaluation
How much grammar did the learners use, and how accurate was it? How easy was it to reformulate some of the learners' language in the way suggested in **9.4**? It would be useful to reappraise this activity a week or so later, eliciting from learners what they recall of the language they used. This would indicate how salient the whole procedure was for them. What modifications would you make for a subsequent but similar activity?

Glossary

bottom-up processing: paying attention to grammar and lexis to make sense of language.

cohesion: linguistic links across sentences or clauses.

consciousness-raising: the degree to which learners are guided to discover aspects of grammar for themselves.

context: the social, psychological, and physical setting in which language use takes place.

context-gap: the gap in knowledge between what is known to be known among all learners at the outset of a task, and what needs to be expressed to complete the task.

discourse: contextualized stretches of language perceived to be meaningful and constructed out of motivated choices.

formal grammar: grammar presented as form in isolation from its meaning in context.

formulaic language: language which learners perceive as fixed expressions.

functional grammar: grammar seen as a system for the expression of meaning.

given–new principle: the tendency for what is introduced at the beginning of a sentence to be given information, and what is at the end of the sentence to be new information.

grammar: the identification of systematic regularities in language.

grammaticization: the process of applying grammar to words in language use.

hypothetical distance: the degree to which states or events are seen as remote from actuality.

idealization: the process of decontextualizing language.

input: the language to which learners are exposed.

intake: language in the input which learners notice.

interlanguage: learner language.

interlanguage stretching: where learners use language to the limit of their current ability.

lexis: vocabulary.

linguistic distance: the quantity of language used to signal a message. The more language, the greater the linguistic distance.

morphology: the systematic modification of words through alteration and addition.

noticing: the conscious intake of new language.

noticing as skill: listening and reading tasks which require attention to grammar in order to comprehend certain meanings.

proceduralization: the process of forming and mentally storing language routines through experience in language use.

process activity: the unregulated production of learner language, where the purpose of the activity is unclear or unidentified.

psychological distance: the degree to which states or events are seen to be relevant and part of the speaker/writer's current mental world.

redundancy (of grammar): where there is no apparent need for features of the grammar to be attended to or used.

reflection activities: where learners consider and evaluate grammar in their own language.

regulation: the careful design of tasks in order to encourage a rich deployment of grammar by learners.

routines: fixed or partially fixed phrases which language users access from memory for efficient language use.

schematic knowledge: knowledge of the way the world is conventionally organized.

shared knowledge: relevant knowledge which is shared between participants in language use.

social distance: the degree of intimacy and directness with which people position themselves and each other in social contexts.

structuring: the progressive sorting out by learners of their knowledge of language into hypotheses about its structure.

syntax: linguistic rules for combining words in sentences.

systemic knowledge: knowledge of the language system.

teaching grammar as grammaticization: providing learners with words to be combined so as to make certain meanings clear.

teaching grammar as process: regulating tasks for language use to encourage the deployment of grammar through self-expression.

teaching grammar as product: focusing learner's attention on pre-specified forms and their meanings.

teaching grammar as skill: carefully guiding learners to attend to grammar while retaining a measure of self-expression and meaning-focus.

top-down processing: making sense of language by primary reference to schematic knowledge.

Further reading

Halliday, M. A. K. 1985. *An Introduction to Functional Grammar* (pages i–xxxv). Edward Arnold.
This is a very clear and eloquent outline of the nature of grammar as a communicative system, including its origins and its potential.

Rutherford, W. 1987. *Second Language Grammar: Learning and Teaching.* Longman.
An important and tightly argued book. Rutherford believes strongly that grammar is intricately connected with discourse—of its nature, in learning, and in language use. This book covers all these areas, and considers applications of this view of grammar for language teaching.

Rutherford, W. and **M. Sharwood Smith** (eds.) 1988. *Grammar and Second Language Teaching.* New York: Newbury House.
A very useful selection of papers, including some important discussion of consciousness-raising and its relevance to the teaching of grammar.

Widdowson, H. G. 1990. *Aspects of Language Teaching.* Oxford University Press.
This is a concisely argued series of essays which covers and extends a number of the key areas discussed in this book, both in terms of theory and of practice. Particularly noteworthy is the paper 'Grammar, nonsense, and learning'.

Bibliography

Abbs, B., and I. Freebairn. 1982. *Opening Strategies (Student's Book)*. London: Longman.

Abbs, B., and I. Freebairn. 1984. *Building Strategies (Student's Book)*. London: Longman.

Anderson A., and T. Lynch. 1988. *Listening*. In the series *Language Teaching: A Scheme for Teacher Education*. Oxford: Oxford University Press.

Anderson, J. 1985. *Cognitive Psychology and its Implications (2nd edn.)*. New York: Freeman.

Azar, B. S. 1985. *Fundamentals of English Grammar*. Englewood Cliffs, NJ: Prentice Hall.

Bell, J., and R. Gower. 1991. *Intermediate Matters (Student's Book)*. London: Longman.

Black, V., M. McNorton, A. Malderez, and S. Parker. 1986. *Fast Forward 1*. Oxford: Oxford University Press.

Bolinger, D. 1975. *Aspects of Language (2nd edn.)*. Harcourt Brace Jovanovich.

Boutin, M. C., S. Brinand, and F. Grellet. 1987. *Writing: Intermediate*. Oxford: Oxford University Press.

Broughton G. 1990. *Penguin English Grammar A–Z for Advanced Students*. London: Penguin.

Brown, G., and G. Yule. 1983. *Teaching the Spoken Language*. Cambridge: Cambridge University Press.

Brown, K. 1984. *Linguistics Today*. London: Fontana.

Brown, P., and S. Levinson. 1978. 'Universals in language usage: politeness phenomena' in Goody 1978.

Bygate, M., A. Tonkyn, and E. Williams (eds.) 1994. *Grammar and the Language Teacher*. New York: Prentice Hall.

Candlin, C. N. 1987. 'Towards task-based learning' in Candlin and Murphy 1987.

Candlin, C. N., and D. Murphy (eds.) 1987. *Language Learning Tasks*. Englewood Cliffs, NJ: Prentice Hall.

Carrell, P. L., and J. C. Eisterhold. 1983. 'Schema theory and ESL reading.' *TESOL Quarterly* 17/4:553–73.

Cook, G. 1989. *Discourse*. In the series *Language Teaching: A Scheme for Teacher Education*. Oxford: Oxford University Press.

Crookes, G. 1989. 'Planning and interlanguage variation.' *Studies in Second Language Acquisition* 11:367–83.

Crookes, G. and S. Gass (eds.) 1993. *Tasks and Language Learning: Integrating Theory and Practice.* Clevedon, Avon: Multilingual Matters.

Day, R. (ed.) 1986. *Talking to Learn: Conversation in Second Language Acquisition.* Rowley, Mass.: Newbury House.

Di Pietro, R. 1987. *Strategic Interaction.* Cambridge: Cambridge University Press.

Doff, A., and C. Jones. 1991. *Language in Use: A Pre-intermediate Course.* Cambridge: Cambridge University Press.

Doff, A., C. Jones, and K. Mitchell. 1983. *Meanings into Words: Intermediate.* Cambridge: Cambridge University Press.

Doff, A., C. Jones, and K. Mitchell. 1984. *Meanings into Words: Upper Intermediate.* Cambridge: Cambridge University Press.

Duff, A. 1989. *Translation.* Oxford: Oxford University Press.

Duff, P. 1986. 'Another look at interlanguage talk: taking task to task' in Day 1986.

Eastwood, J. 1992. *Oxford Practice Grammar.* Oxford: Oxford University Press.

Ellis, G., and B. Sinclair. 1989. *Learning to Learn English: A Course in Learner Training.* Cambridge: Cambridge University Press.

Ellis, R. 1984. 'Can syntax be taught? A study of the effects of formal instruction on the acquisition of *wh*-questions by children.' *Applied Linguistics* 5/2:138–55.

Ellis R. 1985. *Understanding Second Language Acquisition.* Oxford: Oxford University Press.

Ellis, R. 1987. 'Interlanguage variability in narrative discourse: style shifting in the use of the past tense.' *Studies in Second Language Acquisition* 9/1:1–19.

Ellis, R. 1990. *Instructed Second Language Acquisition.* Oxford: Basil Blackwell.

Ellis, R. 1993. 'The structural syllabus and second language acquisition.' *TESOL Quarterly* 27/1:91–113.

Felix, S., and H. Wode. (eds.) 1983. *Language Development at the Crossroads.* Tübingen: Gunter Narr Verlag.

Gass, S., and C. Madden (eds.) 1985. *Input in Second Language Acquisition.* Rowley, Mass.: Newbury House.

Gass, S, and Selinker, L. 1984. *Workbook in Second Language Acquisition.* Rowley, Mass.: Newbury House.

Givon, T. 1979a. 'From discourse to syntax: grammar as a processing strategy' in Givon, T. (ed.) *Syntax and Semantics, Vol. 12: Discourse and Syntax.* New York: Academic Press.

Givon, T. 1979b. *On Understanding Grammar.* New York: Academic Press.

Goody, E. N. 1978. *Questions and Politeness: Strategies in Social Interaction.* Cambridge: Cambridge University Press.

Gower, R. 1987. *Speaking: Upper-intermediate.* Oxford: Oxford University Press.

Grellet, F., A. Maley, and W. Welsing. 1983. *Quartet (Student's Book 2).* Oxford: Oxford University Press.

Haiman, J. 1983. 'Iconic and economic motivation.' *Language* 59/4:781–826.

Halliday, M. A. K. 1978. *Language as a Social Semiotic*. London: Edward Arnold.

Halliday, M. A. K. 1985. *An Introduction to Functional Grammar*. London: Edward Arnold.

Harman, I. P. 1990. 'Teaching indirect speech: deixis points the way.' *ELT Journal* 44/3:230–8.

Harmer, J. 1987. *Teaching and Learning Grammar*. London: Longman.

Hartley, B., and P. Viney. 1979. *Streamline English: Connections*. Oxford: Oxford University Press.

Hutchinson, T. 1986. *Project English 2*. Oxford: Oxford University Press.

Jones, L. 1985. *Use of English: Grammar Practice Activities*. Cambridge: Cambridge University Press.

Kadia, K. 1988. 'The effect of formal instruction on monitored and spontaneous naturalistic interlanguage performance.' *TESOL Quarterly* 22/3:509–15.

Keller, E., and S. T. Warner. 1988. *Conversation Gambits*. Hove: Language Teaching Publications.

Larsen-Freeman, D., and M. Long. 1991. *An Introduction to Second Language Acquisition Research*. London: Longman.

Leech, G. 1989. *An A–Z of English Grammar and Usage*. London: Edward Arnold.

Lightbown, P. M. 1983a. 'Acquiring English L2 in Quebec classrooms' in Felix and Wode 1983.

Lightbown, P. M. 1983b. 'Exploring relationships between developmental and instructional sequences in L2 acquisition' in Seliger and Long 1983.

Long, M. H. 1989. 'Task, group, and task–group interactions.' *University of Hawaii Working Papers in ESL* 8/2:1–26.

Long, M. H., and G. Crookes, 1992. 'Three approaches to task-based syllabus design.' *TESOL Quarterly* 26/1.

McArthur, T. 1984. *The Written Word (Book One)*. Oxford: Oxford University Press.

McLaughlin, B. 1990. 'Restructuring.' *Applied Linguistics* 11/2:113–28.

Nattinger, J. R., and J. S. DeCarrico. 1992. *Lexical Phrases and Language Teaching*. Oxford: Oxford University Press.

Newmeyer, F. 1983. *Grammatical Theory: Its Limits and Its Possibilities*. Chicago: University of Chicago Press.

Nolasco, R. 1987. *Speaking: Elementary*. Oxford: Oxford University Press.

Nunan, D. 1988. *Syllabus Design*. In the series *Language Teaching: A Scheme for Teacher Education*. Oxford: Oxford University Press.

O'Malley, J. M., and A. U. Chamot. 1990. *Learning Strategies in Second Language Acquisition*. Cambridge: Cambridge University Press.

Pawley, A., and F. H. Syder. 1983. 'Two puzzles for linguistic theory: nativelike selection and nativelike fluency' in Richards and Schmidt 1983.

Peters, A. 1983. *The Units of Language Acquisition*. Cambridge: Cambridge University Press.

Prabhu, N. S. 1987. *Second Language Pedagogy*. Oxford: Oxford University Press.

Quirk, R., and S. Greenbaum. 1973. *A University Grammar of English*. London: Longman.

Radley, P., and C. Millerchamp. 1989. *Mode 2*. London: Collins.

Reading and Thinking in English. 1979. Book 2: *Exploring Functions*. Oxford: Oxford University Press.

Richards, J. C., and M. N. Long. 1985. *Breakthrough 3* (New edn.) Oxford: Oxford University Press.

Richards, J. C., and R. W. Schmidt. 1983. *Language and Communication*. London: Longman.

Riddle, E. 1986. 'The meaning and discourse function of the past tense in English.' *TESOL Quarterly* 20/2:267–86.

Rinvolucri, M. 1984. *Grammar Games*. Cambridge: Cambridge University Press.

Rutherford, W. E. 1980. 'Aspects of pedagogical grammar.' *Applied Linguistics* 1/1:60–73.

Rutherford, W. E. 1987. *Second Language Grammar: Learning and Teaching*. London: Longman.

Rutherford, W. E., and M. Sharwood Smith (eds.) 1988. *Grammar and Second Language Teaching: A Book of Readings*. Rowley, Mass.: Newbury House.

Schmidt, R. 1983. 'Interaction, acculturation, and the acquisition of communicative competence' in Wolfson and Judd 1983.

Schmidt, R. 1990. 'The role of consciousness in second language learning.' *Applied Linguistics* 11/2:129–58.

Seliger, H., and M. H. Long. 1983. *Classroom-oriented Research in Second Language Acquisition*. Rowley, Mass.: Newbury House.

Selinker, L. 1972. 'Interlanguage.' *International Review of Applied Linguistics* 10:209–30.

Sharwood Smith, M. 1988. 'Consciousness-raising and the second language learner' in Rutherford and Sharwood Smith 1984.

Shepherd, J., R. Rossner, and J. Taylor. 1984. *Ways to Grammar*. Basingstoke: Macmillan.

Shiffrin, R., and W. Schneider. 1977. 'Controlled and automatic human information processing. 2: Perceptual learning, automaticity, attending, and a general theory.' *Psychological Review* 84:127–90.

Skehan, P. 1994. 'Second language acquisition strategies and task-based learning' in Bygate, Tonkyn, and Williams 1994.

Soars, J., and L. Soars. 1986. *Headway Intermediate*. Oxford: Oxford University Press.

Swain, M. 1985. 'Communicative competence: some roles of comprehensible input and comprehensible output in its development' in Gass and Madden 1985.

Swan, M. 1980. *Practical English Usage*. Oxford: Oxford University Press.

Swan, M., and **C. Walter.** 1985. *Cambridge English Course 2.* Cambridge: Cambridge University Press.

Thomson A. J., and **A. V. Martinet.** 1986. *A Practical English Grammar.* Oxford: Oxford University Press.

Ur, P. 1988. *Grammar Practice Activities: A Practical Guide for Teachers.* Cambridge: Cambridge University Press.

Wallace, C. 1992. *Reading.* In the series *Language Teaching: A Scheme for Teacher Education.* Oxford: Oxford University Press.

Widdowson, H. G. 1990. *Aspects of Language Teaching.* Oxford: Oxford University Press.

Willis, D. 1990. *The Lexical Syllabus: A New Approach to Language Teaching.* London: Collins.

Willis, J., and **Willis, D.** 1988. *Collins COBUILD English Course (Student's Book 1).* London: Collins.

Wolfson, N., and **E. Judd.** (eds.) 1983. *Sociolinguistics and Second Language Acquisition.* Rowley, Mass.: Newbury House.

Yule, G., T. Mathis, and **M. F. Hopkins.** 1992. 'On reporting what was said.' *ELT Journal* 46/3:245–51.

Index

Entries relate to Sections One, Two, and Three of the text, and to the glossary. References to the glossary are indicated by 'g' after the page number.

Acknowledgements

The author and publisher are grateful to the following for their kind permission to reproduce extracts and figures from copyright material:

Cambridge University Press and the authors for extracts and figures from *Cambridge English Course 2* (1985) by M. Swan and C. Walter, *Meanings Into Words (Upper Intermediate)* (1984) by A. Doff, C. Jones, and K. Mitchell, *Language in Use (A Pre-intermediate Course)* (1991) by A. Doff and C. Jones, *Language in Use (Classroom Book)* (1991) by A. Doff and C. Jones, *Use of English: Grammar Practice Activities* (1985) by L. Jones, *Learning to Learn English: A Course in Learner Training* (1988) by G. Ellis and B. Sinclair, *Grammar Practice Activities: A Practical Guide for Teachers* (1988) by P. Ur, and *Grammar Games* (1984) by M. Rinvolucri.

The Guardian for a photograph of protesters from *The Guardian*, 23.6.90.

HarperCollins Publishers Ltd for extracts and figures from *Collins Cobuild English Course, Students' Book 1* (1988) by J. Willis and D. Willis.

Heinle & Heinle Publishers for an extract from P. Duff's article in *Talking to Learn: Conversation in Second Language Acquisition* (Newbury House, 1986) edited by R. Day.

Language Teaching Publications for a figure from *Conversation Gambits* (1988) by E. Keller and S.T. Warner.

Longman Group UK for extracts from *Intermediate Matters* (1991) by J. Bell and R. Gower, *Opening Strategies* (1982) by B. Abbs and I. Freebairn, and *Second Language Grammar: Learning and Teaching* (1987) by W.E. Rutherford, and for figures from *Teaching and Learning Grammar* (1987) by J. Harmer.

The Macmillan Press Ltd for a figure from *Ways to Grammar* (1984) by J. Shepherd, R. Rossner, and J. Taylor.

Thomas Nelson & Sons for extracts from *An A–Z of English Grammar and Usage* (Nelson ELT, 1989) by G. Leech.

Oxford University Press for extracts and figures from *Reading and Thinking in English: Book 2: Exploring Functions* (1980), *A Practical English Grammar* (1986) by A.J. Thomson and A.V. Martinet, *Practical English Usage* (1980) by M. Swan, *Project English 2* (1986) by T. Hutchinson, *Headway* (1986) by J. Soars and L. Soars, *Oxford Practice Grammar* (1992) by J. Eastwood, *Streamline English: Connections* (1979) by B. Hartley and P. Viney, *Quartet (Students' Book 2)* (1983) by F. Grellet, A. Maley, and W. Welsing, *Breakthrough 3* (1985) by J.C. Richards and M.N. Long, *Writing (Intermediate)* (1987) by M.C. Boutin, S. Brinand, and F. Grellet, *Speaking (Upper Intermediate)* (1987) by R. Gower, *Fast Forward 1* (1986) by V. Black, M. McNorton, A. Malderez, and S. Parker, *Speaking (Elementary)* (1987) by R. Nolasco, *The Written Word, Book 1* (1984) by T. McArthur, and *Translation* (1989) by A. Duff.

Penguin Books Ltd for an extract from *Penguin English Grammar A–Z for Advanced Students* by Geoffrey Broughton, (Penguin Books, 1990) copyright © Geoffrey Broughton, 1990.

Prentice-Hall, Englewood Cliffs, New Jersey for a figure from Betty Schrampfer Azar, *Fundamentals of English Grammar 2e*, © 1992.

Rex Features for a photograph of storm damage to telephone boxes.